Abigail's Pa

G000270601

A Play

Mike Leigh

Samuel French – London
New York – Sydney – Toronto – Hollywood

ABIGAIL'S PARTY

First performed at the Hampstead Theatre, London on 18 April, 1977, when the cast was as follows:

Beverly   Alison Steadman
Laurence Tim Stern
Angela   Janine Duvitski
Tony   John Salthouse
Susan   Thelma Whiteley

Directed by Mike Leigh

Designed by Tanya McCallin

In the subsequent revival at the Hampstead Theatre, which opened on 18 July, 1977, and in the television version which was transmitted as a "Play For Today" on BBC-1 on 1 November, 1977, the part of Susan was played by Harriet Reynolds.

The action takes place in Laurence and Beverly's house

ACT I   Early evening in Spring

ACT II Later that evening

Time—the present.

ACT I

The ground floor of Laurence and Beverly's house. An early evening in spring

The floor comprises a living-area, a dining-area and an open-plan kitchen. In the living-area are a three-piece leather suite, an onyx coffee-table and a sheepskin rug. Above the settee is a room-divider shelf unit, on which are a telephone, a stereo system, an ornamental fibre-light, a fold-down desk and, prominently, a bar. The hall and front door are unseen

As the CURTAIN *rises and the Lights come up, Beverly enters. She puts on a record—Donna Summer: "Love to Love you, Baby", then lights a cigarette. She places a copy of "Cosmopolitan" in a magazine rack, then pours a gin and tonic. She goes to the kitchen, gets a tray of crisps and salted peanuts, puts them on the coffee-table, and sits on the settee*

After a pause, Laurence enters with an executive case

Laurence (*kissing her*) Hullo.
Beverly Hi.

Laurence puts his case on the armchair

  You're late.
Laurence Sorry? (*Laurence turns down the music which plays on to the end*)
Beverly I said, you're late.

Laurence pours himself a Scotch

Laurence Yes. Sorry about that—unavoidable.
Beverly What happened?
Laurence Oh, some clients, they were late.
Beverly Laurence, don't leave your bag on there, please.
Laurence I'll move it in a minute.
Beverly D'you get something to eat?
Laurence No.
Beverly No? (*Rising*) I had to throw your pizza away, I'm sorry.

Beverly gets from the refrigerator two small platefuls of home-made cheese-and-pineapple savouries—each consisting of one cube of cheese and one chunk of pineapple on a cocktail stick. Laurence opens the desk, gets his case, opens his notebook, goes to the telephone. Beverly returns and puts the plates on the coffee-table.

Laurence Just got to make a couple of phone calls
Beverly D'you want me to make you a little sandwich?
Laurence No, I must get these out of the way first. (*He stops the record*)

Beverly Laurence, you want to have your bath and get changed: they're going to be here soon.

Laurence Yes.

Beverly sits

(*On the telephone*) Oh, is Mr O'Halligan there, please?... O'Halligan.... Yes. Well, he's big. He's bald, with red hair.... Thank you.

Pause

Beverly Laurence, you're going to get heartburn. *Irony*

Laurence (*on the telephone*) Mr O'Halligan?... Mr Moss here, Wibley Webb. Hullo. D'you realize I've been trying to contact you all afternoon?... I know you've been out! Now, where's that key to Fifteen Clittingham Avenue?... Ah, but you were supposed to have it back before lunch! That's no good, I need it now. Will you be in tomorrow morning?... Tonight! Where?... Belfast? What time's your plane?... All right, train then.... A party? I thought you just said you were going to Belfast!... Well what time are you going to Kilburn?... Well, what time are you having your bath? I'm not asking you to bath in cold water—I just want the key to Fifteen Clittingham Avenue; I've got another client who wants to view the property.... What about you, Mr O'Halligan?... Well, Mr O'Halligan, if you'd like to come in on Monday morning with your deposit, and go ahead and get in touch with your building society, we'll see how things go. Now what about this key?... All right, I will come and get it! Now!

Beverly Laurence—no!

Laurence (*on the telephone*) Yes, I've got the address.... Yes, I know how to get there.... Okay—I'll see you shortly. Good-bye! (*He hangs up*) Stupid man.

Beverly Oh Christ, Laurence.

Laurence What?

Beverly How long's all this going to take, please?

Laurence Oh, yes—I'm sorry. It won't take long. (*He dials another number*)

Beverly D'you get those lagers?

Laurence Er, no, I didn't have time.

Beverly Laurence! (*Pause*) Well, you'd better get them when you go out, and don't forget, please.

Laurence (*on the telephone*) Hullo, Mrs Cushing?... Laurence Moss here, Wibley Webb!... Yes, Mrs Cushing, we have run him to ground, and you'll be happy to know that I'm now in the throes of retrieving the key!

Beverly gets herself another drink

Not at all, not at all—all part of the service!... Ah. Ah, yes—now, when would be best for you?... No, no, I'll fall in with you, Mrs Cushing. How about tomorrow morning?

Beverly Laurence!

Laurence (*on the telephone*) My pleasure, Mrs Cushing, my pleasure.

Now, what time would suit you best?... No, I'm at your service, Mrs Cushing, he who pays the piper calls the tune! You name the hour, and I shall appear!... No, really: I insist.... What time? Eight o'clock? Sure, surely.

Beverly *Laurence.*

Laurence (*on the telephone*) Early? Not at all, Mrs Cushing—up with the lark, you know.... Don't mention it, Mrs Cushing, it's my privilege. 'Bye, Mrs Cushing—see you tomorrow morning! 'Bye now! (*He hangs up*)

Beverly You're going to kill yourself, you know, Laurence.

Laurence Yes. Well it can't be helped.

Beverly It's ridiculous.

Laurence It's not a nine to five job—you know that, Beverly.

Beverly You can say that again.

Laurence sits with Beverly

You gonna get changed?

Laurence Yes. I'll drink this; I'll get changed; then I'll go out.

Beverly And don't forget those lagers.

Laurence Beverly—where are the olives?

Beverly In the kitchen, Laurence. Laurence, if you want olives, would you put them out, please?

The front doorbell chimes

Laurence (*jumping up*) They're early, aren't they?

Beverly No they're not. And you've not changed.

Laurence I know that. (*He goes to answer the door*) Beverly, get the olives.

Laurence exits

Beverly composes herself, then rises, and prepares to receive guests, going to the door

Angela (*off*) Hello, you must be Laurence!

Laurence (*off*) That's right.

Angela (*off*) I'm Angie.

Laurence (*off*) Do go in, won't you?

Angela (*off*) Thank you. This is my husband, Tony.

Tony (*off*) How d'you do.

Laurence (*off*) Hullo.

Angela, Laurence and Tony come in

Beverly Hi, Ang.

Angela Hello, Beverly—what a lovely dress!

Beverly Thanks.

Angela Were we meant to wear long?

Beverly No, no, it's just informal, you know ...

Angela This is my husband, Tony.

Beverly How d'you do, pleased to meet you.

Tony How d'you do.
Beverly He's got a firm handshake, hasn't he? *Flirt w. Tony*
Angela Yes.
Beverly Yeah, fantastic. Like to go through?
Tony Ta.
Angela This is the suite I was telling you about. It's nice, isn't it?
Tony Lovely.
Angela We've just bought a new three-piece suite, but ours isn't real leather, like this—it's "leather look".
Beverly Oh, the Leather Look? Great.
Laurence Drink?
Tony Yes, please.
Beverly Laurence, would you like to take Angela's coat, please?
Laurence Surely.
Angela Thanks.
Laurence Pleasure.

Laurence takes Angela's coat out

Beverly It's funny, 'cos he's a lot bigger than I thought he was. Yeah—'cos I've seen him across the road, Ang, and I thought he was about the same size as Laurence—
Angela Oh, no . . .
Beverly —but he's not, he's a lot bigger, yeah, great. Would you like a drink?
Tony Yes, please.
Beverly What would you like?
Tony Bacardi and Coke, please.
Beverly Ice and lemon?
Tony Yes, please.
Beverly Great, How about you, Ang?
Angela Have you got gin?
Beverly Gin and tonic?
Angela Please.
Beverly Ice and lemon?
Angela Yes, please.
Beverly Great.

Laurence enters

Laurence, would you like to get the drinks, please? Tony would like Bacardi and Coke with ice and lemon, Angela would like gin and tonic with ice and lemon, and I'd like a little fill-up, okay?
Laurence Surely.
Beverly D'you like lager, Tony?
Tony I'll be all right with Bacardi, thank you.
Beverly No—as a chaser, a little bit later on; because Laurence is gonna get some.
Tony It'll be okay, thank you.
Beverly Or a light ale. Which d'you prefer?
Tony Light ale.

Beverly Light ale? Laurence, would you get some light ale as well, please?
Laurence Yes.
Beverly Actually, Ang, it's going to be really nice, because I've invited Sue from Number Nine.
Angela Oh, lovely.
Beverly Yeah, so I thought it'd be nice for you to meet her as well. Yeah, 'cos her daughter's having a party. Well, she's only a teenager, so I said, well pop down and spend the evening with us.
Angela That'd be really nice, 'cos I want to meet all the neighbours.
Beverly Yeah, just say hello, Ang, and break the ice.
Angela 'Cos that was what was so nice when you came over, 'cos it really made me feel at home.
Beverly Well, Ang, I know what I felt like when I moved in—I was lonely. So I thought, well, that's not going to happen to you.
Angela Well, you're the friendly type, aren't you?
Beverly Yeah, yeah. It's funny, 'cos as soon as we met, I knew we were gonna get on.
Angela Well, we're alike, aren't we?
Beverly Yeah, yeah.

Laurence gives Angela and Beverly their drinks

Thanks.
Angela Thanks.

Laurence gives Tony his drink

Tony Thank you.
Beverly Cheers, everyone!
Angela Cheers!
Beverly Cheers, Tone!
Tony Cheers.

Laurence gets his glass from the coffee table

Laurence Cheers!
Angela Cheers!
Beverly What are you doing, darling? Are you staying, or going?
Laurence Er, I'll stay for a while.
Beverly Laurence has to pop out on business, I'm afraid, so . . . Now: anybody like a cigarette? Laurence, would you, please?

Laurence offers the cigarette box

Angela?
Angela No, thanks.
Beverly Tony, would you like a cigarette?
Tony No, thank you.
Angela We've just given up.
Beverly Oh, yeah. Sorry!
Laurence Now, who'd like some olives?

Beverly Not for me. Ang?

Angela No, thanks.

Beverly Tony, d'you like olives?

Tony No, I don't.

Beverly No, they're horrible, aren't they?

Angela Yes.

Beverly They've got a very bitter taste, haven't they, Ang?

Angela Yes.

Beverly I told you nobody'd like olives, Laurence.

Laurence Not nobody, Beverly: I like olives. And that's twenty-five per cent of the assembled company.

Angela We've met you before, haven't we?

Laurence Really?

Angela He is the one you remember, isn't he?

Tony Yeah.

Angela D'you remember us? We came looking for a house.

Laurence I can't say I do; of course we see a lot of clients.

Tony We saw a lot of estate agents.

Angela Yes, we went to all the ones in the area. We got the house from Spencer's in the end—Anthony Spencer.

Beverly Oh, Anthony Spencer, yeah, yeah.

Angela Well it was Nicholas Spencer who was dealing with us.

Beverly Yeah?

Angela He's very nice. D'you know him?

Laurence Yes, I know him.

Angela Have you seen those boards they have outside?

Beverly Ang, aren't they beautiful?

Angela Yes, they're lovely. With the house and the family and the car and the tree. When I saw them I thought, "I hope we get a house with one of those boards." I expect they sell a lot of houses because of the boards. Don't you think so?

Laurence No actually, I don't.

Angela Oh, don't you? We were very lucky, actually, 'cos we got the price of the house down from twenty-two thousand to twenty-one thousand.

Beverly Really? Oh that is fantastic, Ang, that's really great.

During the following, Beverly offers cheese-pineapple savouries to Angela and Tony. So does Laurence, though superfluously as it turns out. Tony says "ta" where appropriate

Is it your first house?

Angela Yes, we were in a furnished flat before.

Beverly Oh, that's a bit grim, isn't it, furnished flat? Yeah.

Angela Yes. Well it was nice for us while we were saving.

Beverly Yeah.

Angela But the trouble is, with it being furnished, it means we haven't got much furniture of our own together yet.

Beverly Yeah, and you feel it when you move, don't you?

Angela Yes.

Beverly (*sitting*) Mind you, Ang, your house is smaller than this one, yeah, because I known they are smaller on your side, yeah.

Angela Yes. Mmm. These are lovely.

Beverly Yes, they're dainty, aren't they? Your bed arrived yet, Ang?

Angela Oh, don't talk about that—it's a sore point.

Beverly Is it?

Angela Well, it's funny, really, 'cos I came back from work today, 'cos I'm not working nights any more, I'm on days.

Beverly Yeah?

Angela And I came home, and I saw this big parcel in the hall, and I saw his face, and he was looking furious, and I thought, What's happened? And you know what? The bed-head had arrived, and no bed.

Beverly No, Ang! Laurence, did you hear that? How many weeks ago is it you ordered that bed, Ang?

Angela Four.

Beverly Four weeks ago they ordered a bed, and it still hasn't arrived. It's disgusting.

Laurence Well, you can't trust anybody these days.

Angela No.

Beverly It's disgraceful. I mean, you've been sleeping on the floor, haven't you Ang?

Angela Yes. Well, we've got a mattress from Tony's mum, but it's not the same.

Beverly No. Well, let's face it, Tone, you can't do much with a bed-head, can you? D'you know what I mean?

Pause

Laurence What line of business are you in?

Tony ⎱ Computers.   ⎰ (*Speaking*
Angela ⎰ He's in computers.   ⎱ *together*)

Beverly Oh, really, Tone? That's funny, 'cos my brother's in computers, actually.

Angela Is he?

Beverly Yeah, he's a—programmes analyst.

Angela Oh yes? Tony's just an operator.

Beverly I know it's a fantastic job, though, Tone, 'cos my brother, he had to go to college and get exams. I mean, he was studying for years, wasn't he, Laurence?

Laurence Oh, yes.

Beverly Did you have to do all that, Tone—go to college?

Angela You didn't really, did you?

Tony No.

Angela No.

Beverly I know it is a fantastic job, though, Tone, 'cos my brother, he's got a fabulous house and he gets great wages, y'know? Yeah.

Laurence Nine to five is it?

Tony No, it's not, actually; there's quite a bit of variation.

Angela Shift-work.

Tony It's a two-weekly system: one week I work from eight in the morning till four in the afternoon, and the following week I work from four till midnight. I get every other Saturday off.

Beverly Oh, great. Were you off today, Tone?

Tony Yeah, I was, actually.

Angela Yes. It's lucky, 'cos if I'm working on a Saturday, he can do all the shopping.

Laurence Oh yes? Where do you shop?

Angela ⎱
Tony ⎰ Sainsbury's.   ⎰ *(Speaking*
                          ⎱ *together)*

Laurence Ah, we usually go to the Co-op. I find they have a much wider range of goods there.

Beverly Don't you find shopping boring, though, Ang?

Angela Mmm.

Beverly Oh, I do—I hate it. He takes me down in the car, and I get me wheely, Tone, and I whizz in, and I grab anything I can see, and I bung it in the wheely, he writes me a cheque, we bung it in the car, bring it home, and it's done for the week, d'you know what I mean?

Laurence Beverly is not very organized: she doesn't believe in making shopping-lists. You have a car, do you?

Tony Yeah.

Angela Yes, an Escort.

Laurence A yellow one?

Angela That's it.

Laurence Yes, I've seen it.

Beverly Yeah, it's beautiful, actually.

Angela Beverly was saying you only like Minis.

Laurence No, not at all. I don't only like Minis—I like lots of other cars. But I find the Mini economical, efficient and reliable, and the most suited to my purposes. Of course, I change my car every year.

Beverly Yeah, but what I say, Ang, is this: what is the point in changing your car if all you change is the colour?

Laurence That's not all you change, Beverly; the design does alter. But then you're not a motorist, so of course you just don't understand these things.

Beverly Yeah, okay. I know I failed my test three times.

Laurence Three times.

Beverly But, I'm his wife, Ang, and I reckon a wife should have a little say in the choosing of a car.

Laurence Well, when you've passed your test, Beverly, then you can have your little say. Until then, please leave it to me.

Beverly Let me put it to you this way, Ang. When we chose the furniture, we chose it together; when we chose the house, we chose it together; but, when it comes to the car, I'm not allowed to have a say.

Laurence goes

Beverly Don't forget those light ales!

Laurence No—and the lagers, yes!

Angela You going to take your test again?

Beverly Yeah, I'm going to have another try, yeah. Don't get me wrong, Tone, it's not that I can't drive—in fact I'm a good driver, but, let me put it to you this way, when I get to my test my nerves fail me, d'you know what I mean? I mean it was me nerves that failed me the last time, to be honest with you, because you know the way they take you out in threes, Tone, right? I started off behind this bloke—he was a Chinese bloke actually. Now, my bloke had told me to turn left, right? Now, we came to the first Give Way, and the bloke in front slammed his brakes on. Now, I'm going behind him, and I suppose I'm going a little bit too quick with me nerves; so I slam on my brakes, and I went slap in the back of him.

Angela Ah.

Beverly Now, I reckon that prejudiced my examiner against me.

Angela What a shame.

Beverly Yeah, it was, actually. Can you drive, Ang?

Angela No. I'd like to learn, but Tony won't let me. He doesn't think I'd be any good. And it's a shame, 'cos it's so awkward for me to get to work since we've moved.

Beverly Is it, yeah?

Angela And you see, I could use the car when he wasn't working.

Beverly And that would make you completely independent of Tone, wouldn't it?

Pause

D'you pass your test first time, Tone?

Tony Yeah.

Beverly I thought so, actually—he looks the type, doesn't he? (*She goes to the bar*) Who's for another drink? Ang?

Angela Thanks.

Beverly How about you, Tone?

Tony Ta.

Beverly Yeah? Great.

Laurence enters

What's the matter?

Laurence Nothing. Tony, I wonder if you could give me a hand for a moment please?

Beverly Won't the car start?

Laurence No.

Angela Go on, Tony!

Tony All right!

Tony follows Laurence out

Beverly Mind you don't go getting dirt on your suit. All right, Tone?

Beverly concludes pouring drinks

Ang.

Angela Thanks.

Beverly Cheers.

Angela Cheers.

Beverly Ang—would you mind if I asked you a personal question?

Angela No.

Beverly Now, please don't be offended when I say this, but, what colour lipstick are you wearing?

Angela A pinky red.

Beverly A pinky red! Now, can you take a little bit of criticism? Please don't be offended when I say this, but, you're wearing a very pretty dress, if I may say so; now, you see that pink ribbon down the front? If you'd chosen, Ang, a colour slightly nearer that pink, I think it would have blended more with your skin tones; d'you know what I mean?

Angela A paler colour.

Beverly A slightly paler colour. Now, can I give you a tip?

Angela (*after a brief pause*) Yes.

Beverly Now, okay. I can see what you've done: you've just sat down in front of your mirror, and you've put your lipstick on. Now, this is something I always used to tell my customers, and it always works. Now, next time, just sit down in front of your mirror, and relax. And just say to yourself, "I've got very beautiful lips." Then take your lipstick and apply it, and you'll see the difference, Ang. Because then you will be applying your lipstick to every single corner of your mouth, d'you know what I mean? Will you try it for me next time?

Angela Yes.

Beverly Just sit down in front of your mirror, and relax, and say to yourself . . .

Angela "I've got very beautiful lips."

Beverly And I promise you you'll see the difference, Ang! Okay?

Angela Thanks.

The front door bell chimes

Beverly Would you excuse me just one minute, Ang?

Beverly goes out

Angela helps herself to a cheese-pineapple savoury

Beverly (*off*) Hi, Sue.

Susan (*off*) Hello, Beverly.

Beverly (*off*) Come in.

Susan (*off*) Thank you.

Beverly and Susan enter. Susan carries her handbag and a wrapped bottle

Beverly All right, Sue?

Susan Yes, thank you.

Beverly Come through.

Susan I'm sorry I'm a bit late.

Beverly Now, don't worry, Sue, that's all right. Would you like to slip your jacket off?

Susan Oh, thank you.

Beverly Everything all right, Sue?

Susan Yes, I think so. I hope so.

Beverly Come through and say hullo. Ang, this is Sue. Sue, this is Ang.

Angela Hello.

Susan How d'you do.

Beverly Sue's from Number Nine.

Angela Oh, we've just moved into Number Sixteen.

Susan Oh, really?

Beverly Yeah, you know the Macdonalds' old house, Sue?

Susan Yes.

Beverly Yeah. Sit down Sue. I'll just pop your coat in the hall. (*Going*) Won't be a sec. Make yourself at home, Sue!

Beverly exits with Susan's coat

Susan Thank you. (*She puts the wrapped bottle on the bar, and proceeds to sit down, putting her handbag on the floor*)

Angela We've only been here a fortnight.

Susan Oh, really?

Beverly returns

Beverly (*referring to the bottle*) Did you bring that, Sue?

Susan Yes.

Beverly Is it for us?

Susan Yes.

Beverly Oh, thank you, Sue!

Susan It's nothing very special, I'm afraid.

Beverly Ah. Isn't that kind, Ang?

Angela Yes.

Susan Not at all.

Beverly (*unwrapping the bottle*) Oh, lovely! 'Cos Laurence likes a drop of wine, actually. Oh, it's Beaujolais. Fantastic! Won't be a sec, I'll just pop it in the fridge. (*She goes to the kitchen*)

Angela I'm so pleased to meet you. I want to meet all the neighbours.

Susan Yes.

Beverly returns

Beverly Now Sue: what would you like to drink?

Susan I'll have a glass of sherry, please.

Beverly Sherry, are you sure?

Susan Yes. Thank you.

Beverly 'Cos we've got everything. There's gin, whisky, vodka, brandy, whatever you'd like. Would you like a little gin and tonic, Sue? 'Cos me and Ang are drinking gin and tonic, actually.

Susan All right—thank you.

Beverly Ice and lemon?

Susan Yes please.

Beverly Great.

Angela It's a nice drink, gin and tonic, isn't it?
Susan Yes, it is.
Angela Refreshing.

Tony enters during the following

Sometimes I drink lager and lime. Say I'm in a pub with my husband, I'll drink that. But I prefer this.
Tony Can I wash me hands, please?
Beverly Yes, just one second, Tone, while I finish making Sue's drink. Sorry: Sue—this is Tony.
Angela My husband.
Susan ⎫ How d'you do.   ⎧ (*Speaking*
Tony ⎭   ⎩ *together*)
Angela Did you push it all right?
Tony Yeah. The battery was flat.
Beverly Sue!
Susan Thank you.
Beverly Cheers.
Susan Oh, cheers.
Beverly Now. Tony, hands! Come through. (*She takes Tony to the kitchen*) Soap and towel there. Okay?
Tony Ta.
Angela D'you work?
Susan No. No. I don't.
Angela I'm a nurse.
Susan Oh.
Angela At St Mary's in Walthamstow.
Susan Oh, yes.
Angela Beverly says your daughter's having a party. Is that right?
Susan That's right, yes.
Angela Has it started yet?
Susan Yes. Yes, it has.
Beverly All right, Tone?
Tony Yes, thank you.
Beverly Come through.

Tony comes through

Drink's on there. Like to sit down?
Tony Ta. (*He sits*)
Beverly Now then, Sue, let's see—would you like a little cigarette?
Susan Oh. No, thank you.
Beverly Are you sure?
Susan Yes, thank you.
Beverly Perhaps you'll have one a little bit later on. And I know Angela doesn't want one. Now, everybody all right?
Tony Yes, thank you.
Angela Yes, lovely, thanks.
Susan Yes. Thank you.

Beverly Yes? Great!

Rock music starts at Number Nine, not especially loud

Beverly Aye aye! It's started, Sue.

Angela They've got the record-player going, haven't they? They're going to have fun, aren't they?

Beverly Sounds like it.

Susan I hope so.

Angela How old is she, your daughter?

Susan Fifteen.

Angela What does she look like? 'Cos I might have seen her.

Susan Oh. Well, she's quite tall, and she's got fair hair, quite long fair hair.

Angela She hasn't got a pink streak in her hair, has she?

Susan Yes.

Beverly Yeah, that's Abigail! And she wears those jeans Ang, with patches on, and safety-pins right down the side, and scruffy bottoms.

Angela Yes, I've seen her.

Susan And plumber's overalls.

Beverly Yeah, plumber's overalls. She makes me die, you know!

Angela I've seen her: she was standing outside your gate with a friend. And you've seen her as well, haven't you? Getting off that motorbike.

Tony Yeah.

Angela How many people are coming to the party?

Beverly About fifteen, isn't it, Sue?

Susan Well, it was fifteen. Then it went up to twenty, and last night I gathered it was twenty-five.

Beverly It's creeping up, Sue.

Susan I've told her that's the limit. Well, I think that's enough. Don't you?

Beverly Definitely, Sue, yeah, definitely.

Angela Yeah.

Beverly But, this is it with teenagers: okay, they tell you twenty-five; but a friend invites a friend; that friend invites another friend; and it creeps up till you end up with about seventy or eighty. This it is. This is the danger!

Tony I've just seen a couple of people arriving, actually.

Susan Yes. Nice of them to help you with the car.

Tony Oh, no—not them—a couple of coloured chaps and a girl roared up in a Ford Capri.

Susan Oh, really? (*Pause*) Well, there were only half a dozen there when I left—when I was asked to leave.

Beverly Yeah, this it it, isn't it? They don't want Mum sitting there, casting a beady eye on all the goings-on, do they?

Angela No. Not when they get to fifteen. When I was fifteen I really wanted a party of my own, and my Dad, he'd never let me. You see, I've got four sisters. Haven't I, Tony?

Tony Yeah.

Angela And I think he was a little bit worried that I'd invite all my friends and they'd bring along a few of theirs, and we'd end up with a houseful.

Beverly This is it.

Angela And he was worried about people pinching things, and things getting broken.

Beverly Have you locked your silver away, Sue?

Susan No I haven't got any. Well not much, anyway. I've put a few things upstairs; just in case of accidents.

Angela Yes, well it's better to, isn't it? 'Cos it can easily happen.

Beverly Yeah.

Angela (*to Tony*) Like that egg-timer. (*To Beverly and Susan*) Tony was furious. It was a wedding present.

Beverly Don't get me wrong, Sue: I wasn't meaning that any of Abigail's friends are thieves—please don't think that. But, you don't know who you get at a party. And let's face it—people are light-fingered.

Angela Yes.

Pause

Beverly D'you leave your carpets down, Sue?

Susan Er—yes.

Angela Have you got fitted carpets?

Susan Yes.

Angela Yes—we've got fitted carpets. The Macdonalds' left them all. They were inclusive in the price of the house.

Susan Oh?

Angela And we're very lucky, because we got the price of the house down from twenty-two thousand to twenty-one thousand.

Susan Really?

Angela I don't know what we'll do about our carpets when we have a party. 'Cos we're having a party soon, aren't we?

Tony Housewarming.

Angela Yeah. You'll have to come.

Susan Thank you.

Beverly This is it, though, isn't it, with fitted carpets, you don't know what to do for the best. Particularly with teenagers. Because let's face it, they're not as careful as, say, we would be, d'you know what I mean, they don't think; I mean, they've got a drink in one hand, a cigarette in the other, they're having a bit of a dance, and the next thing you know is it's cigarette on your carpet, and stubbed out.

Angela Is it your daughter's birthday?

Susan No. She just wanted a party. No particular reason.

Beverly Yeah, well, they don't need a reason these days, do they? Any excuse for a bit of a rave-up—what do they call it, freak out? D'you get that beer, Sue?

Susan Yes. I got four of those big tins, and some Pomagne.

Angela Oh, that's nice, isn't it?

Susan Yes it is.

Beverly It's funny, at that age we used to drink Bulmer's Cider. We used to say, "A glass of cider, and she's anybody's."

Angela I got very drunk on champagne at our wedding. D'you remember?

Tony Yeah.

Beverly Gives you a terrible headache, champagne doesn't it?

Angela Yes. In the morning.

Beverly Yeah, shocking. D'you get any spirits, Sue?

Susan No. No, I didn't.

Beverly No. You're very wise. 'Cos they're so expensive, aren't they? And let's face it, if they want to drink spirits, they can bring their own. Particularly the older boys. 'Cos they're working, aren't they? I mean, there will be older boys at the party, won't there?

Susan Oh, yes.

Beverly Yeah. Well, let's face it, Ang, when you're fifteen you don't want to go out with a bloke who's fifteen, do you?

Angela No.

Beverly 'Cos they're babies, aren't they? I mean, when I was fifteen, I was going out with a bloke who was twenty-one.

Pause

How's Abigail getting on with that bloke, by the way, Sue?

Susan I'm not sure—I daren't ask.

Beverly Mind you, I reckon you're better to let her go out with as many blokes as she wants to at that age rather than sticking to the one. Don't you agree with me, Ang?

Angela Yes. How many boy-friends has she got?

Susan I don't know. I don't think she really knows herself.

Angela Footloose and fancy free!

Beverly Actually, Sue, I was just thinking—it might be a good idea if a little bit later on, if Laurence and Tony pop down there. Now I don't mean go in; but just to check that everything's all right; put your mind at rest. Don't you agree with me, Ang?

Angela Yes, it's a good idea. You don't mind, do you?

Tony No.

Susan It's very nice of you. But I don't think it'll be necessary.

Tony Your husband's away, then, is he?

Susan No. We've split up, actually.

Angela Are you separated, or divorced?

Susan Divorced.

Angela When did you get divorced?

Susan Three years ago.

Angela Oh well—that's given you time to sort of get used to it, hasn't it? We've been married three years—three years in September, isn't it?

Beverly Yeah, me and Laurence have been married three years, actually.

Angela Oh, it's funny—we were all getting married about the same time as you were getting divorced!

Susan What a coincidence.

Angela Yes! Where is he now? D'you know?

Susan Yes. He lives quite near here, actually.

Angela Oh, that's nice. D'you keep in touch?

Susan Yes.

Beverly Yeah, he pops over to see the kids, doesn't he, Sue?

Susan Yes. He comes every Sunday.

Angela Does he?

Susan For lunch.

Angela Ah, lovely. Is he coming tomorrow?

Susan I expect so.

Angela Ah, that's nice—for the kids.

Beverly Yeah, well, let's face it, Sue, whatever you say about him, he is their father, isn't he?

Susan Yes.

Beverly Mind you, I don't believe in people sticking together for the sake of the kids. To me, that is wrong. I mean, take my parents, for example. Now, you might not believe this Sue, but it's the truth. My parents have not spoken to each other for twenty years, and as long as I can remember my father has slept in the boxroom on his own.

Angela Yeah, well that's like my father—he's terrible to my mother.

Beverly Is he?

Angela He hardly speaks to her.

Beverly Yeah. You see, it's not fair, is it Ang? I mean, take my mum, right? She's sixty and she's ever so sweet—she wouldn't hurt a fly. But, she's really ill with her nerves. And why? It's a result of all the rows that have been going on.

Angela Yes, well that's like my mum. She's been very ill for five years, seriously ill with a blood disease.

Beverly Ah!

Angela She might die at any moment.

Beverly Really?

Angela But it doesn't make any difference: my dad's still as rotten to her as he's always been.

Beverly Is he? Yeah, you see, it's not fair, is it? I mean, this is the truth: if my father was to drop dead tomorrow, I wouldn't care. 'Cos I hate him. We all hate him. But, he's the kind of bloke, he'll live till he's ninety. Whereas your mum, bless her, she could do with her good health, and she hasn't got it. Now to me, it's all wrong. I mean, they say The Good Die Young, and I'm afraid it's true.

Angela Yeah, well it's like Tony's dad. He just walked out and left Tony's mum, and you were only about three, weren't you?

Tony You like living round here, do you?

Susan Yes. It's a very pleasant area.

Pause

Angela What did your husband do?

Susan He's an architect.

Angela Oh, that's a good job, isn't it?

Susan Yes, it is.   } *(Speaking*

Beverly Yeah, it's a good job, architect.   } *together)*

Angela Well paid.

Susan Yes, it can be. It's quite a long training, though.

Angela Yes.

Beverly Has David married again, Sue?

Susan Yes.

Angela Oh, well—it's a good job that he's got a good job, then, isn't it? I mean, if he's got two families to support.

Beverly Have they got any children, Sue?

Susan No. But she wants some. So they're trying. But they don't seem to have had any success so far.

Angela Does she come over on Sundays?

Susan No, he comes on his own.

Angela Oh, but I suppose like, when your kids go over there, it's nice for her 'cos she's got a little ready-made family.

Susan Well, they don't go over there, actually. Well, hardly ever.

Angela Don't you get on with her?

Susan No. Well—I hardly know her, really.

Angela Well, I mean—if your husband runs off with another woman, well . . .!

Beverly (*going to the bar*) Well, let's face it, Ang, you can hardly be the best of mates, can you, d'you know what I mean?

Angela No.

Beverly Now, would anybody like another drink? Ang?

Angela Thanks.

Beverly Sue?

Susan I still have some, thank you.

Beverly Yeah, come on, Sue, I'll just give you a little top-up. That's it. Now, Tone, another drink?

Tony Ta.

Beverly pours drinks during the following

Angela I think more and more people are getting divorced these days, though.

Beverly Yeah, definitely, Ang. Mind you, I blame a lot of it on Women's Lib. I do. And on permissiveness, and all this wife-swapping business. Don't you, Tone?

Tony I suppose so.

Beverly Don't you, Sue?

Susan Possibly.

Beverly I mean, take Peter Sellers for example. Now he has been married at least five or six times.

Susan Four, actually.

Beverly Is it four, Sue?

Angela Well, look at Elizabeth Taylor and Richard Burton.

Beverly Now to me, their relationship is ridiculous. I think they make a mockery of marriage. I think it's disgusting.

Angela They only do it for the publicity.

Beverly I mean, with these film stars, I reckon half the time the attraction is purely physical.

Angela They did it in the jungle.

Beverly Yeah. I mean, to a film star, getting divorced is like going to the lavatory, if you'll pardon my French. But to us, it's a big wrench, isn't it, Sue?

Susan Yes, of course.

Angela Yes.

Susan But I think that film stars only get married because the public expects it.

Beverly Do you?

Susan Yes. I do.

Angela I think people take divorce for granted I think if they stuck it out, they'd be all right, don't you?

Beverly Yeah. But, mind you, there are times, Ang, let's face it, when you could hit them on the head with a rolling-pin, and clear out. D'you know what I mean?

Angela Yeah, well that's like Tony and me. I mean we've only been married nearly three years, but we're always having rows, aren't we?

Tony Yeah.

Beverly (*handing Tony his drink*) She give you a bad time, Tone?

Tony (*taking his drink*) Ta. Shocking.

Angela And I think it spoils things, doesn't it?

Susan Yes. it does.

Beverly Mind you, I reckon a little row sometimes adds a sparkle to a relationship. You know.

Angela Did you have a lot of rows with your husband?

Susan No, we didn't actually.

Angela Oh.

Beverly Well, there you go, you see, it doesn't always follow. It's funny, isn't it? D'you think people should get married, Tone?

Tony Sometimes.

Angela Oh, he's not so sure, you see, since he's been married to me!

Beverly Perhaps we should all live in sin, and forget the whole thing, I don't know.

Angela Did you live with Laurence before you got married?

Beverly No, I didn't, actually.

Angela D'you think if you had have done, you'd still have married him?

Beverly No, I don't honestly think I would have done. Don't get me wrong: I do love Laurence, in my own way. But, if we'd have lived together, say for a year, I don't honestly think it would have worked out.

Pause

Tony I think if you're going to have kids you ought to get married.

Beverly Oh yeah, definitely, Tone, give them a name, yeah.

Angela Yes.

Beverly You'll be having all this soon, Sue. Do you think Abigail is the marrying type?

Susan I hope so.

Angela Oh, you'll probably be getting married again yourself soon!

Susan Oh, I don't think that's very likely.

Angela You never know. 'Cos I never thought anyone would marry me. And you see, I met Tony, and we were married within a year, weren't we?

Tony Eight months.

Angela Yes. So you see, it can happen.

Susan Really?

Angela Have you got a boy-friend?

Susan No.

Pause

Beverly Would you like to have kids, Ang?

Angela Yes. Yes, I would.

Beverly Would you, Tone?

Tony Not for a while.

Angela Not till we get settled in.

Beverly Yeah, get yourself sorted first, yeah. He'd make a nice dad, though, wouldn't he?

Angela Yes.

Beverly I could just see you, actually, with a little boy—you know: taking him out, and looking after him!

Angela Be nice to have one of each.

Beverly Yes, like Sue. It's funny, though, with Sue's kids, to me, Abigail and Jeremy aren't a bit alike. Are they, Sue?

Susan No. They're not.

Beverly They're like chalk and cheese, Ang.

Angela Do they take after you or your husband?

Susan Neither of us, really. Jeremy looks more like my brother. Abigail doesn't look like anyone in the family.

Beverly The Black Sheep. Eh, Sue—how did Jeremy get on packing his little overnight bag?

Susan Oh, he loved it!

Beverly Did he? Yeah! You know what kids are like, Sue was telling me, he was so excited about packing all his little things.

Susan He'd have taken the kitchen sink, if I'd let him.

Angela Where's he gone?

Susan Round the corner.

Tony How old is he?

Susan Eleven-and-a-half.

Pause

Angela Would you like kids?

Beverly No, I don't think I would, actually. Don't get me wrong, it's not that I don't like kids, 'cos I do, but, let me put it to you this way: I wouldn't like to actually have to have them. I mean—did you have your kids in hospital, Sue?

Susan Yes.

Angela Did you have an easy labour?

Susan Well—Abigail was really very difficult. But Jeremy was fine. He was born very quickly.

Beverly Yes, you see, to me, having to go into hospital would be like being
ill, and I couldn't stand that. And I know it sound horrible, but all that
breast-feeding, and having to change nappies, would make me heave.
I don't honestly think I've got that motherly instinct in me.

Angela You see it'd be different for me, 'cos I'm used to looking after
children.

Beverly Yeah.

Angela And if I can look after a wardful of sick children, I can easily
manage a couple of my own.

Beverly Yeah.

Angela Because the thing is, with children that are ill, is, that you've got to
watch them every minute. Like, recently, we had this little girl, she was
only about two, and she kept picking at her dressing. She picked it all
off, and got right down into the wound . . .

Beverly I'm sorry, Ang, but would you stop? It's just that if you carry on,
I'll faint.

Tony Leave it out, Ang!

Angela No, it's all right, 'cos she wasn't in any pain, but she actually
got the stitches . . .

Tony Drop it!

Pause

Angela Did you know my husband used to be a professional footballer?

Beverly Really?

Angela Yes, he used to play for Crystal Palace, didn't you?

Tony Yeah.

Beverly Oh, that is fantastic.

Angela That was before I met him.

Beverly What, d'you used to play for the reserves, Tone?

Angela Oh, no; it was the first team.

Beverly Honestly, is that true?

Tony Yeah.

Beverly You're not kidding me?

Angela No.

Beverly What, honestly, the first team?

Tony For a bit, yeah.

Beverly Oh, that is fantastic. Hey, Sue, we didn't know we had a celebrity
moved into Richmond Road, did we?

Susan No, we didn't.

Beverly That is fantastic, Tone: that's really made my night, actually.

*Laurence enters. He stops, registers suddenly remembering something,
curses silently, spins round, and rushes out*

Beverly Laurence! (*She gets up*). Would you excuse me a minute? (*Going*)
Laurence!

Beverly exits

Pause. Abigail's music can still be heard

Angela Nice music. Isn't it Tony?

Pause. Tony gets up and picks up a plate of cheese-pineapple savouries

Tony (*to Susan*) Would you like one of these?
Susan Thank you.

Angela gestures for one. He gives her one silently

Angela Ta. I shouldn't be eating these. 'Cos we had a big tea. Did you eat earlier?
Susan Er—no. No, I didn't.
Angela Oh, you must be hungry. Here, have some peanuts.
Susan (*taking some*) Thank you.
Angela Are they having a barbecue?
Susan No.
Angela Oh, 'cos it's a nice idea, that, if you've got a big garden.
Susan Yes, it is.
Angela I'd love to have a barbecue–you know, do baked jacket potatoes...
Susan Lovely...
Angela Have sausages and chops. And you can do chestnuts. And have an ox—you know, on a spit!

Beverly enters

Beverly Hey, it's all happening at your place, Sue. Oh, it's so funny, Ang. You know your bay window, Sue, at the front? Well it's wide open, and there's this bloke, Ang, he's gotta be twenty stone, and he's wedged in your bay window. He's got one of those purple vests on, you know? —and a great big fat belly. And there's a girl, Sue, standing in your front garden, she's as thin as he's fat, and she's draped round him like this, Ang, and they're snogging away—you've never seen anything so funny in all your life!
Susan Oh, dear.
Beverly Now—don't worry, Sue, 'cos they're only having a bit of fun. I mean, they're only teenagers, aren't they?
Susan I wonder if I dare just pop down there for a minute.
Tony Would you like me to go and have a look for you now?
Susan Er, no.
Angela } Tony doesn't mind.   } (*Speaking*
Tony } It's no problem.   } *together*)
Susan No—thank you—but I think perhaps it's better not.
Beverly No, Sue's right. It's best not to pop down there. They're only having a bit of fun. And let's face it, when Laurence gets back we can discuss it then. Okay? Now, who's for another drink? Come on Ang!

Angela joins Beverly at the bar

How about you, Sue?
Susan No, thank you.
Beverly Yeah, come on, Sue, give you a little top-up, just to settle your nerves. That's it. How about you, Tone? Another drink?

Angela is wandering round the room

Tony Ta. Where is Laurence, anyway?

Beverly I don't know, actually, Tony. I wish I did know.

Angela Oh, what a lovely table. This is just what we need. It's the next thing we're going to get. 'Cos at the moment we're eating off our knees. It's unusual, isn't it—with the wooden top and the modern legs?

Beverly Yeah, it was expensive, that one, actually.

Angela Yes. (*Looking at a candelabra*) Ah, and this is what I'd really love!

Beverly What, the candelabra? Yeah, it's brilliant, isn't it?

Angela Yes. Is it real silver?

Beverly Yeah, silver plate, yeah.

Angela Yes. And it looks so lovely, and with the light.

Angela wanders into the kitchen. Beverly gives Susan her drink

Beverly Sue.

Susan Thank you.

Beverly You all right, Sue?

Susan Yes, fine, thank you.

Beverly Yeah. (*Pause*) Sue you must think I'm dreadful! I do apologize: I haven't offered you anything to eat. I'm sorry! Have some nuts.

Susan Thank you.

Beverly Take some crisps, as well.

Susan Thank you.

Beverly Now then, Sue, let's see—would you like a little cheesy-pineapple one?

Susan Thank you.

Beverly Tone? A little cheesy-pineapple one?

Tony Ta.

Beverly Take another one, Sue—save me coming back.

Susan Thank you.

Beverly Now then, Sue—a little cigarette?

Susan No, thank you, not just at the moment.

Beverly Sorry, Sue—I'll tell you what I'll do: I'll pop it on here for you, Sue, and then you can light it when you've finished those. Okay? Lovely.

Angela (*from the kitchen*) Tony, come and have a look at this beautiful kitchen.

Beverly It's lovely, isn't it?

Angela Oh, these tiles are gorgeous. Were they here when you came?

Beverly Yeah, we were lucky, actually.

Angela You were. 'Cos our kitchen's nothing like this. Tony, come and have a look.

Beverly Yeah, go and have a look, Tone, they're beautiful, actually; go on—go and have a look.

Angela Tony!

Beverly Go on.

Tony goes to the kitchen

Angela Is this a freezer part with your fridge?

Beverly Yes, it's a freezer at the top, yeah. (*To Susan*) He's nice isn't he?
Susan Yes.
Beverly Yeah, he's fantastic. Yeah—they're a very nice couple, actually; aren't they?
Susan Yes.
Angela Oh, the sink's got its own light.
Tony Leave it!
Angela And you've got one of these!
Beverly ˙What, the rôtisserie? Yeah.
Angela D'you cook chickens and things on it?
Beverly (*joining Angela and Tony*) Well, you can do, but to be honest I'm not much of a cook, so I haven't actually used it yet. And you can also do kebabs, they're very nice.

Laurence enters with a carrier bag

Angela Oh, lovely.
Beverly Would you excuse me, Tony? (*She leaves the kitchen*)
Laurence Oh, hullo Sue. You all right?
Susan Yes, fine, thank you.
Beverly Laurence, where have you been, please?
Laurence To the off-licence.
Beverly Those want to go in the fridge, Laurence, to chill. Sorry, Ang, sorry, Tone—come through!
Angela Thanks.

Laurence takes the lagers to the kitchen

Beverly Like to sit down?
Tony Ta.

Angela and Tony sit down, Angela on the settee

Beverly Now then, Sue, let's see—that little cigarette . . .
Susan Oh, thank you. (*Sue takes cigarette left for her earlier*)
Beverly (*lighting Sue's cigarette*) There we are, Sue.
Susan Thank you.
Beverly Now; everybody all right?
Angela ⎱ Yes thanks.   ⎰ (*Speaking
Tony ⎰ Yes, thank you.   ⎱ together*)
Susan ⎰ Yes . . . thank you. ⎱
Beverly Great.

Beverly collects her drink and sits. Laurence returns from the kitchen. Pause.

Laurence Right now, who's for a drink? Tony, light ale?
Tony Not just yet, thank you.
Beverly Go on, Tone, have a light ale, 'cos he got them specially for you.
Laurence If he doesn't want one, he doesn't have to have one, Beverly. Sue?
Susan No, thank you.
Laurence Angela?

Angela No, I'm all right, thanks.
Laurence Beverly?
Beverly No, I'm fine thank you.
Laurence Laurence? Yes, please. (*He gets his glass*) Thanks very much.

Only Angela laughs. Laurence pours his drink

Well, the party certainly seems to be hotting up at your place, Sue.
Susan Yes—so Beverly said.
Beverly Yeah, we were just saying, actually, Laurence, it might be a good idea if a little bit later on, if you and Tony would pop down there.
Laurence What for?
Beverly Just to check that everything's all right, for Sue—put Sue's mind at rest. Because I know she's a little bit worried.
Susan I think it'll be all right.
Laurence Yes, Sue, I don't think there'll be any problems.
Susan No.
Beverly Laurence, I'm not saying there'll be any problems—all I'm saying is, would you please pop down for Sue?
Angela You don't mind do you, Tony?
Beverly No, of course he doesn't mind.
Tony No, I don't mind.
Laurence Well, I've just been past, and everything seems to be all right.
Angela Didn't you see what was happening in the garden?
Laurence Well—yes . . .
Angela The couple, snogging through the window?
Laurence Through the window?
Angela With the dirty vest?
Laurence No. No, I saw a couple down the side of the house, and there were a few in the porch. But I didn't see anybody in the window.
Tony Would you like to sit down here, Laurence?
Laurence No, no—you stay where you are.
Angela No, sit here—there's plenty of room.
Laurence Thank you.

Laurence sits on the settee between Angela and Susan

Laurence Anyway, Sue, these sort of things, they nappen at parties.
Susan Yes, of course.
Laurence I'm sure it's nothing to worry about.
Susan No.
Beverly Actually, Laurence, I think you're being very unfair to Sue.
Susan Oh, not at all.
Beverly Now, Sue, don't make excuses for him. And apart from anything else, Tony has already agreed to go actually.
Laurence Oh, have you?
Tony Yeah.
Laurence Yes, well, I didn't say I wouldn't go. If she wants us to go down there, surely, of course we'll go.
Susan Well, I don't know that I do, really.

Laurence Fine.
Angela Tony doesn't mind going on his own, do you?
Tony No, I don't.
Laurence I didn't say I wouldn't go.
Beverly Fine, then, Laurence, are you going, please?
Laurence Yes.
Beverly Thank you.
Laurence That's quite all right.

Pause

Beverly I'm not saying there'll be any trouble, but, with teenagers, they
    have a drink, and they get over-excited—
Angela Yes, well it starts with one kiss . . .
Beverly —then they find their way to the bedrooms.

Pause. Sue flicks ash from her cigarette

Laurence Sue, do you like olives?
Susan Yes.
Laurence (*getting up*) Fine. I'll get you some!
Susan Thank you.

Laurence goes to the kitchen

Beverly You've got a friend for life there, Sue.
Susan Oh?
Beverly None of us like olives, you see.
Susan Ah, I see.
Beverly I can't stand them. It's those stuffed olives—you know that little
    red bit that sticks out? Well, it reminds me of—well, I'm not going to
    say what it reminds me of, but I can't eat them, it puts me off.

Laurence returns with the olives

Laurence Sue?
Susan Thank you.

*During the following Laurence sits between Susan and Angela, and eats a
couple of olives. After a while he starts looking for something in his pockets*

Angela Well, not everyone can like everything, can they? It's like Tony, he
    dosen't like curry, and I love it. So we never go to Indian restaurants
    now, do we?
Tony No.
Angela And you can get English food in Indian restaurants—I mean you
    can have chips with your meal instead of rice. But you see Tony had a
    bad experience in an Indian restaurant—this was before I knew him—
Beverly Yes?
Angela He had a nasty dose of gastro-enteritis after he'd had a curry, and
    you see that put him off.
Beverly Yes.
Angela And he won't even eat curry at home, now. Which is a shame,

because I enjoy making it; it's a good way of using up leftovers. Have
you ever tried pilchard curry?

Beverly No.

Angela That's a very economical dish. And it's easy: just get one of those
big tins of pilchards in tomato sauce, and mix it with curry powder and
onions, and it's really tasty.

Beverly Oh?

Angela I used to share this flat with these girls, and we often used to do that.
But you see, Tony won't touch it. But then, I don't like Turkish Delight,
and you see, Tony loves that.

Laurence still searches in his pockets

Beverly (*to Laurence*) Darling, have you got heartburn?

Laurence No.

Beverly Have you got heartburn?

Laurence No, I haven't got heartburn. (*He gets up and goes to his case*)
Just a slight case of indigestion, that's all.

*During the following, Laurence gets out an antacid tablet and eats it. Then
he gets out a small cigar*

Beverly I thought so. This is it, you see, Ang. He came in late, and he
was all upset; 'cos he's very highly strung, Sue, and this gives him heartburn.

Angela Ah, he must be careful then; because when I was working in
intensive care, the people who'd had a cardiac arrest, they were nearly all
business men, and those who were worrying about their work.

Beverly I hope you're listening to this, Laurence.

Laurence Yes, I'm listening! Cigar?

Tony No, thank you. I've just given up.

Laurence Are you sure?

Beverly Yeah, go on, Tone, take a little cigar, enjoy yourself, go on, take
one!

Laurence Yes, go on, take one.

Tony Thank you. (*He takes one*)

Angela Tony! Oh well, that counts doesn't it? I mean, if he's having a
cigar . . .

Beverly Yeah, come on, Ang!

Angela takes a cigarette

Laurence Sue—

Angela Thanks!

Laurence —would you like one?

Susan Er—no, thank you.

Laurence Some women do like them, you know, Sue?

Susan Yes, so I understand, but I've got a cigarette.

Laurence Oh. (*To Tony*) Light?

Tony Ta.

Angela 'Course, smoking's one of the chief causes of heart disease.

Susan But it's just contributory, isn't it?

Angela Well, yes, but if somebody's got a tendency towards that condition, they really shouldn't smoke.

Laurence No, no, no. I don't believe that smoking, in moderation, can do any harm at all.

Beverly Laurence would you like to put a record on for us, please?

Laurence Yes, surely; what would you like to hear?

Beverly Feliciano.

Laurence Oh, no, Beverly. (*Going to the records*) We don't want to listen to that blind Spaniard caterwauling all night.

Beverly Darling, not classical.

Laurence Light classical—just as a background. (*Producing a record*) Sue, d'you know James Galway?

Susan Yes, I've heard him.

Laurence He's a very up-and-coming young flautist. Do you like him?

Susan Yes, he's very good.

Laurence Fine, I'll put it on for you.

Beverly Laurence, I'm sorry, but we don't want to listen to classical music at the present moment.

Laurence Well, what do you want to listen to, then, Beverly?

Beverly Feliciano.

Laurence Well, if everybody wants to listen to Feliciano, we'll put it on.

Beverly Tone, d'you like Feliciano?

Tony Yeah, I do.

Beverly Yeah, he's fantastic, isn't he? Sue?

Susan I don't know him, I'm afraid.

Angela Oh, you'll like him. He's lovely.

Beverly Yeah, Sue, he's really great. Sue, would you like to hear him?

Susan Yes.

Beverly Yeah? Laurence, Angela likes Feliciano. Tony likes Feliciano, I like Feliciano, and Sue would like to hear Feliciano: so please, d'you think we could have Feliciano on?

Laurence Yes.

Beverly Thank you.

During the following, Laurence puts on the record—Jose Feliciano: "California Dreamin' "

Angela Oh, it changes colour, doesn't it?

Beverly What, the fibre-light? Yeah! Isn't it beautiful, Ang?

Angela Oh, it's lovely!

Beverly Yeah. D'you know what I do, Ang? I put a record on and I sit in that chair, and I just gaze at it for hours.

Angela Do you?

Beverly Yeah. It's funny, it always reminds me of America. I don't know why, but it does.

Pause

Angela Oh yes, it's New York, isn't it?

Beverly Yes, I suppose it is, really . . .
Angela How are you enjoying your cigar?
Tony Very nice, thank you. How's your cigarette?
Angela Oh, it's lovely. Mind you don't choke on it! You see, he's not used
   to smoking a cigar—he doesn't know what to do with it.
Beverly He'll be all right. Tone, would you like another drink?
Tony Ta.
Beverly Yeah? How about you, Ang?
Angela Please.
Beverly (*taking her glass*) Thanks. Sue?
Susan Oh, no, thank you.
Beverly (*taking Sue's glass*) Yeah, come on, Sue—I'll give you a little
   top-up. That's it.

Beverly is joined at the bar by Tony. The music is just about starting.
During the following, Laurence returns to sit between Angela and Susan

Beverly Like to help yourself, Tone?
Tony Ta.
Beverly It's a fantastic drink, Bacardi, isn't it?
Tony Yeah.
Beverly Yeah.
Tony I first started drinking it when I went to Majorca.
Beverly You've been to Majorca?
Tony Yeah.
Beverly Ah, great. Where d'you go?
Tony Palma.
Beverly Not Palma Nova?
Tony That's right, yeah?
Beverly Oh, fantastic—isn't it beautiful there?
Tony Yeah.
Beverly They drink it very long there, don't they, with lots of ice and Coke
   and all that, yeah. It's my dream, actually, just lying on the beach,
   sipping Bacardi and Coke.
Angela Have you always had a moustache?
Laurence What d'you mean?
Angela Have you had it for a few years?

Beverly hands Susan her drink

Susan Thank you.
Laurence Yes.
Angela Never thought of having a beard to go with it?
Laurence No.
Beverly No, Laurence wouldn't suit a beard, Ang, his face is too small.
Laurence Actually, I think a beard can look very scruffy.
Angela Yes, but I think a man with a moustache and a beard, they look
   more masculine.
Beverly Sexier, isn't it?
Angela Mmm. Has your husband got a beard?

Susan No, no. He used to have—a long time ago—when I first knew him.
Angela Why did he shave it off?
Susan Well, he grew out of it.

Pause

Laurence Do you play any instruments yourself, Sue?
Susan No. No, I used to play the piano when I was a child.
Laurence Oh, the piano?
Susan Just a little.
Laurence I once went for guitar lessons—but I never kept them up.
Susan That's a pity.
Laurence Yes, I've often regretted it.

Pause

You know, I think that musicians and artists, they're very lucky people; they're born with one great advantage in life. And d'you know what that is? Their talent. They've got something to cling to. (*Pause*) I often wish I'd been born with that sort of talent. (*Pause*) Most people, they just drift through life, without any real aims. They're weak. It's no good just sitting there, whining. You've got to get up, and do something about it. Not that it isn't a fight. Of course it is. Life is a fight—people always seem to be against you. Not that I've done badly—oh, no: I've done all right. But it's certainly an uphill battle.

Angela I once went to a party, and they said, "Can anyone play the piano?" And I said, "Oh, yes, I can." And you see, I can't play the piano—I'd just learned this one tune from a friend. It was—
"Buy a broom
Buy a broom
Buy a broom,
And sweep the room!"
And that's all I knew. And you see, they wanted me to play for musical chairs. So I started:
"Buy a broom
Buy a broom . . ."
And I played it a few times.

Beverly Yeah?

Angela And then I thought, well I'll have to do something a little bit different. So I started, y'know, just . . .

Beverly What, vamping?

Angela Yeah.

Beverly Yes.

Angela But as I can't play, it sounded terrible. And I felt such a fool. I thought, why did I say, y'know, I'd play?

Beverly When was this, Ang?

Angela Oh, it was only when I was eight.

Beverly Oh, I see!

Angela Oh, yes, I still felt a fool, though.

Beverly Would anybody mind if I turned this next track up? Because it's

my favourite, it's "Light My Fire", and I'd like us all to hear it. Anybody
mind?

Angela   ⎱   ⎰ (*Speaking*
Tony   ⎬ No.   ⎨ *together*)
Susan   ⎰   ⎱
Beverly No? Great. (*She turns the record up*) Fantastic, isn't he?
Angela Yeah. I know this one.
Beverly Yeah? D'you think he's sexy, Ang?
Angela Yes. But it's a pity he's blind.
Beverly Yeah. Mind you. I reckon that makes him more sensitive. D'you
know what I mean?
Angela Mmm. Yes.

Beverly proceeds to dance solo in front of the others, and across the room

Beverly D'you like him, Tone?
Tony Yeah.
Beverly Knockout, isn't he? (*She continues dancing, helping herself to a
crisp as she passes by the coffee-table*) This used to turn me on at parties,
Tone, eight years ago—that's how long I've liked him. (*More dancing*)
Ang, imagine making love to this? D'you know what I mean?

Angela laughs

(*Squeezing Laurence's shoulder*) Are you all right, Laurence?

*Beverly dances away from the others with her back to them. Laurence
suddenly jumps up, rushes to the stereo and turns it off*

Laurence Are you ready, Tony?
Beverly Thank you, Laurence!
Laurence Don't mention it. (*To Tony*) Are you ready?
Tony What for?
Laurence Well, Sue wants us to go and inspect the party; I think we
should go and inspect it.
Beverly Fine, Laurence. Would you like to go now, please?
Laurence ⎱ I am going.   ⎰ (*Speaking*
Susan   ⎰ Oh but, I really think it would be better ...   ⎱ *together*)
Beverly It's all right, Sue.
Laurence Are you coming, Tony?
Tony I think so.
Laurence Well, come on, then!

Laurence goes

Tony gets up to follow

Susan I really think it would be better if you didn't.
Tony It's all right. Just take a walk past your house: put your mind at rest.
Beverly Don't worry, Sue; Tony'll handle it.
Tony Won't be long.
Beverly Take care.

Tony exits

Pause

I'm sorry about that.
Angela Oh, that's all right. Shall I put the record on again?
Beverly No, don't bother, Ang, because he's spoilt it now.
Angela Oh, and you were enjoying yourself!
Beverly Yeah, well we were all enjoying ourselves, weren't we? (*Pause*)
To be quite honest, he's a boring little bugger at times, actually. (*Pause*)
Anyway, sod him. Come on, let's all have a drink!
Angela Yeah.
Beverly Come on, Sue!
Susan Oh, no, really . . .
Beverly (*taking Susan's glass*) Yeah, come on, Sue, that's it!

Angela joins Beverly at the bar

I'll tell you what, let's all get pissed. Yeah!
Angela Yeah. We can enjoy ourselves.
Beverly Yeah. Cheers, Ang!
Angela Cheers!
Beverly Cheers, Sue.
Susan Thank you.
Angela Cheers!
Susan Cheers.
Beverly Come on, Ang, have a little cigarette while he's gone, sod him.
Angela Oh, yeah, while he's out.
Beverly Yeah, come on. That's it.

Beverly and Angela light their cigarettes

Susan I think I'm going to be sick.
Angela Are you? Come along, then.
Beverly Come on, Sue.

Susan rises, holding her glass

Angela Where's the toilet?

Angela and Susan move on their way out of the room

Beverly Under the stairs, Ang, in the hall. Take deep breaths, Sue.
Angela Hold on a minute.
Beverly Take deep breaths: you'll be all right.

Susan and Angela exit

Pause

Angela (*off*) That's the way. Bring it all up. That's it. Better out than in.

Beverly reacts, as the Lights fade, and

the CURTAIN *falls*

ACT II

The same. A little later

Beverly has put on the lights. As the CURTAIN *rises she is alone, pouring drinks. Angela enters*

Angela She'll be all right now.

Beverly Yeah, she'll be all right, Ang.

Angela I've just left her on her own for a minute, to sort herself out.

Beverly Yes. She's been sick, hasn't she?

Angela Yes.

Beverly Yeah. And I'm making her a little black coffee, Ang, so that'll help to revive her a little bit, you know?

Angela Mmm.

Beverly Cheers, Ang.

Angela Cheers!

Beverly Cheers!

They drink. Abigail's music can still be heard

Angela I think she's had a few too many gin and tonics.

Beverly So do I.

Angela And on an empty stomach.

Beverly Really?

Angela Oh, yes—she's not had anything to eat tonight.

Beverly Now, she's silly, isn't she? She should have had a meal.

Angela Yeah, well we had a big meal earlier on.

Beverly Yeah, well, I had a meal.

Angela We had lamb chops.

Beverly Did you? Yeah, I had a little frozen pizza.

Angela And she's trying to keep up with us.

Beverly Yeah, yeah; and another thing, Ang, I think she's the type, her nerves, give her a nervous stomach. She has a few drinks, and that makes her sick.

Angela I knew that, and I thought, that's what brought this on.

Beverly Yeah. And it's a shame, 'cos she's ever so nice, isn't she?

Angela Yes.

Beverly Yeah.

Angela I feel a little bit sorry for her.

Beverly So do I, Ang.

Susan enters, carrying her glass

Angela All right?

Susan Er—yes—thank you.

Beverly All right, Sue?—ah, come through. That's it. She still looks a little bit pale, doesn't she, Ang?

Angela Yes. (*Taking Susan's glass*) I'll take that.

Susan Thank you. Sorry.

Beverly Don't worry, Sue. (*Going to the kitchen*) That's all right.

Angela Come and sit down. (*She sits Susan down on the armchair*). That's it. You sit down here. And your soda-water's there. Now, lean forward a minute, lean forward. (*She props an extra cushion behind Susan's back*). That's it. Lovely.

Beverly (*coming from the kitchen with a cup of coffee*). Now look, Sue, I've made you a little black coffee, now I've made it nice and strong, and I haven't put any milk in it, case that makes you sick again. All right?

Susan Actually, I think it would be better if I didn't.

Beverly Are you sure, Sue?

Susan Yes.

Beverly Oh, all right, then, I'll tell you what I'll do: I'll pop it on here for you. Now, will you try and sip that for me, Sue?—because it will help to revive you. All right? (*She puts the cup on the coffee table*).

Angela Have you got a headache?

Susan Yes, just a bit.

Beverly Would you like a little Aspro, Sue?

Susan Oh, no, thank you.

Beverly Are you sure?

Susan Yes.

Angela No, she's better just with soda-water, 'cos she'll only bring it up.

Beverly I've got it! Just a minute; let's see. (*Looking in her handbag*) Yeah, here we are. Now look, Sue, this is only a very light perfume . . .

Susan I'm all right, actually!

Beverly (*applying perfume to Susan's face*) Now, Sue, it will just help to freshen you up a little bit. Because when you've been vomiting, Ang, you feel horrible, don't you?

Angela Yeah.

Beverly Yes. That's it. (*Applying some to her own hand*) It's lovely, actually. It's Estee Lauder, "Youth Dew".

Angela Mmm.

Beverly Would you like to try some, Ang?

Angela Oh, yes!

Beverly Yeah.

Angela helps herself to a liberal dose

You only need a little drop, Ang!

Angela Oh.

Beverly 'Cos it's quite strong, actually, yeah. That's it.

Angela Mmm, it's nice.

Beverly Yes, it's beautiful, isn't it? Now does that feel a little bit fresher, Sue?

Susan Thank you.

Beverly Yeah?

Pause

Susan Sorry about that.

Angela Oh, there's no need to be sorry, is there?

Beverly Sue—don't worry. Let's face it, it could happen to any of us, couldn't it?

Angela Yes, and it's better for it to happen while those two are away.

Beverly Definitely, yeah.

Susan I wonder—could you pass me my handbag, please?

Angela Yes, where is it?

Susan It's um, on the floor.

While Angela gets the handbag, Susan removes the cushion from behind her

Angela Here we are.

Susan Thank you. (*She takes out a tissue*)

Beverly No, 'cos when you're vomiting in front of blokes, Ang, it's embarrassing, isn't it?

Angela Yes. And they're not usually that sympathetic.

Beverly No.

Angela Well, I know Tony isn't. 'Cos if I've got a headache, or my period pains, he doesn't want to know.

Beverly Really?

Angela In fact, it annoys him.

Beverly Now, this is it, you see; I reckon a woman, she needs a bit of love and affection from a bloke. Okay, sex is important. But, Ang, it's not everything.

Angela No. You see, if Tony comes home, and he's in a bad mood, I can't do anything right. 'Cos they pick on you, don't they?

Beverly Is he like that?

Angela Oh, yes, he's very quick-tempered.

Beverly Is he?

Angela Yes.

Beverly Yeah. It's funny, isn't it, Sue? To see him, sitting there, he looks ever so quiet and gentle, doesn't he?

Susan Yes.

Beverly Is he very violent?

Angela No, he's not violent. He's just a bit nasty. Like, the other day, he said to me, he'd like to sellotape my mouth. And that's not very nice, is it?

Beverly It certainly isn't, Ang!

Angela Was your husband violent?

Susan No, not at all. He was a bit irritable sometimes, a little difficult. But—I think we all are.

Angela Ah! She's one of the lucky ones, isn't she?

Beverly Definitely, Sue, definitely.

Angela Mind you, if Tony wasn't around, I'd miss him.

Beverly Would you?

Angela Yes.

Beverly Yeah. It's funny, isn't it? I suppose I would miss Laurence inasmuch as I need a bloke—well, let's face it, we all need a bloke, don't we? And, okay, credit where it's due: he's very good with money. I mean, if I want a new dress, make-up, have my hair done, whatever it is, the money is there. But, apart from that, it's just boring, know what I mean?

Angela Yes. Well, I think that comes from being married, doesn't it?

Beverly Do you?

Angela The fun wears off.

Beverly Yeah.

Angela Oh, your cushion's slipped.

Susan I'm all right, actually.

Angela Come on, lean forward.

Beverly Yeah, come on, Sue.

Angela Make you comfy.

Beverly 'Cos Angela knows.

Laurence enters

Angela Everything all right down there?

Laurence Yes, I think so.

Beverly How many's at the party, then?

Laurence Well, I don't know—I didn't stop to count them. (*To himself*) This is my glass. (*He goes to the bar*)

Susan It's all right, is it?

Laurence *Yes!* Oh, I'm sorry, Sue. Yes, yes, I went in, and I had a few words with them, and everything seems to be all right.

Angela Where's Tony got to?

Laurence Perhaps you'd better ask him that, when he gets back.

Susan Did you see Abigail?

Laurence I certainly did.

Susan Is she all right?

Laurence I think so.

Angela Where is he?

Laurence Well, I don't know. I'm not his keeper.

Susan Did you talk to her?

Laurence Well, I asked her to turn the music down, yes.

Angela (*to Beverly*) He's stayed at the party!

Susan Was she upset?

Laurence I don't think so.

Beverly (*to Angela*) He's probably being raped by a load of fifteen-year-old schoolgirls!

Angela Oh, lucky them!

Beverly I'll tell you something: at least they had a bit of taste—they didn't pick him. (*She indicates Laurence*)

Angela I hope he's feeling a bit more enthusiastic than when I leap on him!

Beverly Is he one of those?

Angela Yes, he turns over.

Beverly I've met those before, actually.

Laurence (*going to his case for an antacid tablet*) Beverly!

Beverly Ang, I can just see it, right, the music's thumping away and your
Tone's lying on the floor, and there's all these girls, right, you know,
piling on top of him, and your Tone just turns over, and goes to sleep.

Laurence That's enough, Beverly!

Beverly Oh Christ, Laurence! Every time I'm enoying myself . . .!

Laurence Can't you see you're embarrassing Sue?

Beverly Oh, now I'm sorry, Sue. Now, listen, I didn't mean to embarrass
you, Sue; it was only a little joke; all right?

Angela You see, Sue's not been feeling too good, anyway.

Beverly No.

Laurence Oh, really? What's been the problem, Sue?

Susan   ⎱ Oh, it was nothing.   ⎰ (*Speaking*
Beverly ⎰ She's been vomiting, actually.   ⎱ *together*)

Laurence That's all right, thank you, Beverly! Sue can speak for herself!

Angela You see, she's had a few too many gin and tonics, and you've not
had any tea, have you?

Susan No.

Beverly No.

Laurence (*offering her a cheese and pineapple savoury*) Well, would you like
one of these, Sue?

Susan Er, no thank you.

Beverly Laurence, she doesn't want one of those on an empty stomach,
now does she?

Laurence A sandwich, then. Would you like a sandwich, Sue?

Susan No, thank you.

Beverly Laurence, she doesn't want a sandwich!

Laurence Well, *I* want a sandwich! Now do you want a sandwich, Sue,
yes or no?

Susan No. Thank you.

Laurence Okay. Fine!

Laurence rushes to the kitchen, and starts to make a sandwich

Beverly I hope it chokes you!

*Laurence rushes back from the kitchen, with a kitchen knife in one hand,
and a tub of margarine in the other*

Laurence (*pointing the knife at Beverly*) What did you say, Beverly?

Beverly (*shrieking*) Oh Christ, Ang, I'm going to get stabbed.

Laurence Don't tempt me.

Beverly Well, go on, then—do it!

Pause. Beverly pushes away the knife

Beverly Laurence, would you please go back in the kitchen, and finish
making your little sandwich, all right?

Pause

Laurence Are you sure you don't want a sandwich, Sue?

Susan Yes. Thank you.
Laurence Fine.

Laurence goes back to the kitchen. Pause. The front door bell chimes.
Angela and Beverly shriek with renewed mirth

Angela Oh, he's here at last. They must've let him out!

Laurence goes out to the front door

Beverly They've obviously had their fill!
Tony (*off*) Everything all right?
Laurence (*off*) What d'you mean?
Tony (*off*) I wondered where you'd got to.
Laurence (*off*) Yes, well I wondered where you'd got to. Come in.
Tony (*off*) What's that for?
Laurence (*off*) I'm making a sandwich! Go in.

Laurence returns to kitchen. Tony enters and stops by the bar. He looks
slightly flushed and dishevelled

Angela Where've you been?
Tony Southend.
Angela Did you enjoy yourself there?
Tony Wonderful!
Angela Where've you been?—Laurence has been back ages.
Tony (*to Susan*) Everything's all right—nothing to worry about!
Susan Good. Not too rowdy?
Tony No.
Susan Thank you.
Tony It's all right.

Beverly joins Tony near the bar

Beverly Would you like a drink?
Tony Yes, please.
Beverly What would you like?
Tony Light ale, please.
Beverly Like a little Bacardi to go with it?
Tony No, thank you.
Beverly Are you sure?
Tony Yeah.
Beverly Are you all right?
Tony Yeah.
Beverly Great! (*She fixes the drink*)
Susan Was Abigail all right?
Tony I think so.
Susan You saw her?
Tony I didn't actually see her, but I think she's all right.
Beverly (*giving him his drink*) Tone.
Tony Ta.

Beverly Your shirt's all wet.
Angela What is it?
Tony Nothing.
Beverly (*feeling his chest*) But you're soaking wet!
Angela (*getting up*) What've you been doing?
Tony Nothing.

Angela feels his chest

Get off! (*To Susan*) I just bumped into somebody accidentally—minor
incident: nothing to worry about.
Beverly D'you want to sit down, Tone?
Tony Ta. (*He sits*)
Angela Laurence didn't come back with his shirt all wet, did he?
Beverly Dead right he didn't. Laurence comes back looking like he's
spent a day at the office.
Angela I don't think you two have been to the same party, have you?
Tony 'Course we've been to the same party. What are you talking about?
Beverly Ah, lay off her, Tone—she's only having a little joke.
Angela See what I mean?
Tony What?

Susan gets up

Beverly Are you all right, Sue?
Susan Yes. But I think I'd better go and see Abigail myself.
Beverly No, Sue, please. Don't go down there. Now, listen to me, Sue:
you know what Abigail is like, now, she's only going to shout at you,
and then you'll be upset. Now please, Sue, come on, sit down. Now look,
Tony's only just come back—now, it was all right, wasn't it, Tone?
Tony Oh, yeah.
Beverly Yeah?
Tony There's nothing to worry about.
Susan Are you sure?
Tony Yep.

*Laurence returns from the kitchen, having made his sandwich, and sits at the
dining-table to eat it*

Beverly Yeah—now come on, Sue, sit down. Now I'll tell you what I'll do,
I'll put a little record on for us, eh? Yeah! Then we can all have a little
listen to that, yeah. Now, let's see what we've got . . . Tell you what now,
look, Sue—d'you like Elvis?
Susan Yes, he's all right.
Beverly Yeah, he was great, wasn't he! D'you like him, Ang?
Angela Mmm.
Beverly Yeah. Now we'll put this on for Sue.

Beverly puts on the record—Elvis Presley: "Don't"

Angela Is Abigail always having parties?
Susan No.

Pause

Beverly Ready, Ang?
Angela Mmm.

The music starts

Beverly Oh, isn't he great?
Angela Yeah!
Beverly Yeah. (*Pause*) I won't be a sec, I'm just going to the toilet, all right?

Beverly exits giving Laurence a squeeze as she passes him at the dining-table

Long pause. Laurence gets up, adjusts his dress, and goes to the stereo. He turns down the volume

Laurence That's better. Now at least we can hear ourselves think.
Angela D'you want to sit here? (*She indicates the settee*)
Laurence No, thank you.
Angela Come on . . .
Laurence *No thanks!*
Tony Steady!

Pause

Laurence I expect you've seen a few changes since you've been here, eh, Sue?
Susan Not really, no.
Angela When did you move here?
Susan In nineteen sixty-eight.
Angela Oh, you've been here a long time, then, haven't you?
Susan Yes.
Angela D'you think you'll stay here?
Susan Till the children are older.
Angela Oh, yes, then I suppose when you're on your own, you'll get somewhere a little bit smaller?
Susan Yes, I expect so.
Laurence Oh come on, Sue—surely you must have seen some changes?
Susan Well—there are the new houses on the other side of Ravensway.
Laurence Ah, yes, the houses! But what about the people?
Susan What about them?
Laurence The class of people, now don't you think that's changed?
Susan Not really, no.
Laurence The tone of the area—don't you feel it's altered?
Susan Not particularly.
Laurence You don't think it's gone down?
Susan No.

Pause

Laurence And you, Tony, yes, come on, what do you think, eh?
Tony I wouldn't know, would I?

Laurence Oh, no—of course! You've only just moved in yourselves, haven't you?
Angela Yes.
Tony Yes.
Laurence Yes! Drink?
Tony No, thank you.
Laurence Angela?
Angela Please.

Laurence takes Angela's glass, and proceeds to fix her drink

Susan It's more mixed, that's all.
Laurence Mixed? Yes, I suppose you could say it was mixed! More cosmopolitan.
Susan There's nothing wrong with that.
Laurence Oh, you don't think there's anything wrong with that?
Susan No, I don't.
Laurence Well, that's a matter of opinion. Would you like another drink, Sue?
Susan I'm just drinking soda-water, thank you.
Laurence Fine. Would you like some more soda-water?
Susan Thank you.
Laurence (*getting Susan's glass*) We like to keep our guests happy. (*Fixing Susan's drink*) Do you read, Tony?
Tony Sometimes.
Laurence (*giving Susan the drink*) Sue.
Susan Thank you.
Laurence Have you read any Dickens?
Angela Oh, yes. I've read *David Copperfield*.
Laurence *David Copperfield*? Well, I have the Complete Works here. (*He takes one book out, and displays it*)
Angela Oh, they're a lovely set, aren't they?
Laurence (*demonstrating the book*) Yes, they are very well bound. They're embossed in gold.
Angela Mmm—really nice.

Laurence displays it briefly to Tony; then goes over to Sue for a demonstration

Laurence Sue.
Susan Very nice.

Laurence shows Sue the pages, then offers it to her

Laurence Please!
Susan (*taking the book*) Thank you!
Laurence And just what do you read, eh, Tony?
Tony All sorts.
Laurence All sorts! Well, for instance?
Angela What was that one you were reading?
Tony *Computer Crime*.

Laurence *Computer Crime!* Ooh, that sounds interesting. D'you know Shakespeare? (*He goes to his set of Shakespeares*)

Tony Not personally. I read it at school, yeah.

Laurence Oh, at school!

Beverly enters and sits down

Laurence takes out one volume, demonstrates it, then selects a page

Macbeth. (*Pause*) Part of our heritage. (*Pause, he puts it back*) Of course, it's not something you can actually read. Sue?

Susan (*returning the Dickens*) Thank you.

Laurence replaces the Dickens

Angela (*to Susan*) Your house is a lot older than ours, isn't it?

Susan Yes.

Laurence Sue—nineteen thirty-six. Yes?

Susan I'm not sure. But it was built before the war.

Laurence I thought so.

Angela Oh, there's nothing wrong with an old house. I mean, there's some quite nice ones. I like old and I like new. I like those old Tudor houses round here.

Laurence No, Angela. Mock-Tudor.

Angela Are they?

Laurence Oh, yes, There are some real Tudor properties in Hadley Village itself. But the ones you're thinking of are Mock-Tudor.

Angela The trouble with old houses is they haven't got any central-heating.

Laurence Ah, yes, but of course central-heating can be installed into older properties. It may cause some shrinkage of the beams, etcetera, but, if it's done by an expert, there shouldn't be any problems. D'you know the Belvedere Hotel?

Angela Yes. Yes, I do.

Laurence Yes, well, originally, on that site stood a Tudor mansion.

Angela Oh, it doesn't look very old.

Laurence No, no, the present property is late Victorian—neo-Gothic. No, no, the original building, the mansion house, was Tudor. They owned all the land round here.

Beverly D'you want another, Ang?

Laurence I've seen to the drinks, thank you, Beverly!

The following dialogue runs simultaneously with the preceding passage, and starts after Laurence's line, "It may cause some shrinkage of the beams"

Beverly You all right, Sue?

Susan Yes, thank you.

Beverly You don't feel sick again, do you?

Susan No.

Beverly No.

Susan No. It seems to be settling.

Beverly Good. You all right, Tone?

Tony Yes, thank you.
Beverly Great.

Beverly gets up and goes over to Tony

D'you want a drink?
Tony Ta.
Beverly D'you want another, Ang?
Laurence I've seen to the drinks, thank you, Beverly!
Beverly Oh, I'm sorry, Laurence, it's just that I can't hear through two
   brick walls.

Beverly goes to the bar

Laurence Yes, er—it was all part of the Belvedere Estate.
Beverly Laurence, would you like to turn that record up, please?
Laurence How can we hold a conversation with that racket blaring out?
Beverly Laurence, we're not here to hold conversations, we are here to
   enjoy ourselves. And for your information, that racket happens to be
   the King of Rock'n'Roll.
Laurence Oh, really? Well I always thought Bill Haley was the King
   of Rock'n'Roll!

*Beverly turns the volume up. Laurence turns it off. Beverly goes to turn it on;
Laurence grabs her arm. Pause. They are locked together*

Beverly All right, Laurence.

Pause. He lets her go. Pause.

Laurence (*to the others*) Sorry about that.
Angela Oh, that's all right. We're all getting a little bit merry, aren't we?
   And it's nice for us to have a chance to enjoy ourselves, 'cos since the
   move, we've hardly been out.

Susan gets up

Beverly (*sharply*) Where are you going, Sue?
Susan Er—I'm just going to the toilet.
Beverly You don't feel sick again, do you?
Susan No, I'm fine, thank you.
Angela D'you want me to come with you?
Susan (*going*) No, thank you.

   Susan exits

Beverly Give us your glass, Ang. I'll give you a little top-up.
Angela You see, Sue's been vomiting up her gin, and while you were away,
   I had to take her to the lavatory.
Beverly (*giving Angela her drink*) Ang.
Angela Thanks.
Beverly Cheers, everyone. Cheers!
Angela Cheers!
Laurence Cheers.

Tony (*miming his glass*) Cheers!
Beverly Oh, I'm sorry, Tone, I forgot your light ale, didn't I? I do apologize.
Laurence I'll get it.
Beverly Thank you, Laurence!

Beverly sits. Pause

Ang, shall we have a little dance?
Angela Yeah. Be nice.
Beverly Tone, d'you fancy a little dance?
Tony Yeah, I don't mind.
Beverly Yeah?
Laurence There's no room to dance in here, Beverly.
Beverly Laurence, if I'd wanted somebody to put a damper on the idea, I would have asked you first, okay? Come on, Ang, give us a hand moving the couch. Come on.

Laurence gives Tony his drink

Tony Ta.

Beverly and Angela prepare to move the settee

Beverly Got it?
Tony ⎫ It's all right, Beverly, I'll do that. ⎰ (*Speaking*
Laurence ⎭ I'll do it, Angela. ⎱ *together*)

The men take over

Angela I'll take this end.
Laurence No, you just sit down.
Beverly Cheers, Tone.
Tony You got it, Laurence?
Laurence Yes.

Tony and Laurence pick up the settee. Laurence drops his end

Beverly Oh, for Christ's sake, Laurence!
Laurence Don't interfere, Beverly. You ready?
Tony Where d'you want to put it?
Laurence (*to Beverley*) Well, where d'you want it?
Beverly Oh, for God's sake—just put it back there!
Laurence Just back.

Tony and Laurence move the settee

Beverly Ang, I've got this fantastic record I'm gonna play for us, right? Just hang on a sec. Now, this record, Ang, it turns my husband on, and when he hears it, he cannot resist my charms.

Beverly proceeds to put on the record: "Blue Mist", by Sam—The Man—Taylor and his Orchestra

Angela (*as Beverly puts on the record*) They're still enjoying themselves down there, aren't they?

Tony Yes.
Angela What were they getting up to?
Tony Nothing much.
Beverly Ready, Ang?
Angela Mmm.

The music starts

Beverly Fantastic, isn't it? Oh, I'm sorry, Laurence, is it too loud for you,
my darling? I do apologize. I'll turn it down. Because we don't want to
upset him, do we Ang? (*She turns down the volume*) Is that better?
Fancy a little dance, Tone?
Angela Dance with Beverly.
Tony Perhaps Laurence'd like to dance?
Beverly No, I don't think he would, actually. Come on, Tone—have a
little dance, go on.

*Tony gets up and dances with Beverly. Angela and Laurence remain seated
Susan enters—after a few moments*

Beverly You all right, Sue?
Susan Yes. Fine, thank you.

Susan sits. Pause. Beverly and Tony continue to dance

Beverly You don't mind me mauling your husband, do you, Ang?
Angela No, you go ahead.

Pause

Tony (*to Angela*) Go on—dance with Laurence.
Angela No, I can't.
Tony 'Course you can: get up and dance!
Beverly Don't worry, Ang—you'll be quite safe with Laurence. He won't
rape you.

Angela gets up

Angela Would you like to dance?
Laurence (*getting up*) Surely, if you'd like to.

*Laurence places his glass on the coffee-table, and joins Angela; just as he
reaches her, she starts "bopping", which is inappropriate, as the music is
"smoochy", and Beverly and Tony are "smooching". Laurence musters the
vague gesture of a "bop"*

Angela (*whilst dancing*) I'm not very good at these slow dances.
Laurence No.
Angela I'm better at this sort. (*She demonstrates a quick "bop". To Susan*)
Would you like to dance with us?
Susan Oh. No, thank you.
Angela Come on—we can all three dance together!
Susan No, really, I'm fine, thank you.

The dancing continues until the track ends

Laurence (*shaking Angela's hand*) Thank you.

Angela Laurence was shaking my hand!

Beverly Was he? Christ, he'll be shaking mine next. Now who'd like a drink? Ang?

Angela Oh—please!

Beverly Never say no! Tone, would you like a drink?

Tony No thanks, I'm all right.

Beverly How about you Sue?

Susan No, thank you.

Beverly Are you sure?

Susan Yes.

Beverly Yeah!

Angela He's a good dancer, isn't he?

Beverly He's fantastic.

Angela I never knew you could dance so well. We don't usually dance like that, do we?

Tony No.

Beverly (*giving Angela her drink*) Ang!

Angela Thanks.

Beverly Cheers, everyone, cheers!

Tony
Angela } Cheers! { (*Speaking together*)

Susan (*getting the soda-water*) Cheers.

Beverly Darling, why don't you dance with Sue?

Laurence I really don't know that Sue wants to dance, thanks very much. Darling.

Beverly Then why don't you ask her, Laurence?

Pause. Then Laurence gets up and crosses to Sue

Laurence Sue, would you like to dance?

Susan Er, no thank you.

Laurence There you are—Sue doesn't want to dance!

Beverly Of course she wants to dance! Go on, Sue, have a little dance with Laurence. Enjoy yourself, go on—have a little dance.

Laurence Would you like to, Sue?

Susan All right.

Laurence I'll take your glass for you.

Laurence and Susan embrace formally. Beverly rejoins Tony

Beverly Come on. Tone.

Beverly and Tony go into a more intimate embrace than previously

Ang—d'you wanna dance with Tone?

Angela No: you're all right.

Pause. The dancing continues

Laurence Are you going on holiday this year, Sue?

Susan I hope so.

Laurence Expensive business, holidays.
Susan Yes.
Laurence D'you know Paris?
Susan A little.
Laurence Oh. You've been there?
Susan Yes, A long time ago. Have you?
Laurence No. We're hoping to get there.

Pause

Susan I like Paris.
Laurence Oh, yes—Montmartre by night, the Champs Elysées, boulevard
    cafes . . .

When the track ends, they stop dancing. Laurence shakes Susan's hand briskly
and formally

    Thank you.
Beverly (*to Tony*) Thanks very much.
Tony Ta.

They all drift to seats except Tony. The empty seat is now between Susan
and Beverly on the settee

Beverly D'you wanna sit down, Tone?
Tony Ta.
Beverly Ang, do us a favour, throw us me fags. Would you, please?

Angela throws the cigarettes. Tony picks them up and gives them to Beverly

    Cheers, Tone.

Tony leans back. The bar-flap now protrudes over the back of the settee

Susan Mind your head.
Angela It's too big.
Tony What?
Angela It's too big.
Tony What is?
Angela Your head.
Tony Give it a rest!

Pause

    Feeling better now, are you?
Susan Oh—much. Thank you.
Tony Good.

Pause

Beverly Ang, d'you want a cigarette?
Angela Oh, I would. Can I have a cigarette?
Tony D'you want one?
Angela I'd love one.
Tony Why don't you have one, then?

Beverly throws a cigarette across to Angela. She lights it

Beverly Ang, do us a favour—give us a light, would you, please?

Angela goes over to light Beverly's cigarette. She returns

Angela You see, once you've had one cigarette, you want to keep on smoking, don't you?

Beverly This is it, yeah.

Susan What sort of work d'you do?

Tony I'm in computers.

Angela He's an operator.

Beverly Still play football, Tone?

Tony No ...

Angela No, he gave it up when he was twenty. He plays for the firm's team, though; and he's so much better than all the others. *(Starting speaking together)*

Tony It's not the firm's team, and I've only played twice!

Angela He looks so funny in his shorts!

Beverly Why d'you give it up?

Tony Things didn't work out.

Angela You've got footballer's legs, though, haven't you?

Beverly Has he? Have you? Let's have a little look. Oh yeah, so he has. I like footballer's legs, actually—they're nice and muscley, aren't they? Can't stand blokes with skinny legs, Ang, can you? Puts you off—d'you know what I mean?

Laurence Talking of Paris, Sue, do you like art?

Susan Er—yes.

Laurence So do I. Beverly doesn't. Of course, Paris is the centre of the art world. D'you like Van Gogh?

Susan Yes.

Laurence *(crossing the room)* This is a Van Gogh.

Susan Yes.

Laurence They called him a Post-Impressionist, but to my mind he was more of a symbolist. D'you like the Impressionists?

Susan Yes.

Laurence Oh, you do? That's good. Fine. Fine. *(He crosses back to his seat, and sits)*

Beverly You all right, Tone?

Tony Yeah!

Beverly Great.

Laurence Of course, you know, Van Gogh was a very unstable man. Not only did he cut his ear off and leave it in a brothel, he also ate paint, and he shot himself.

Beverly Thank you, Laurence! We don't want all the gory details.

Laurence I'm talking to Sue, and Sue is interested in these things. *(He rushes across the room, and takes the Van Gogh off the wall)* This is a picture of his chair in the corner of his room at Arles. It wasn't actually yellow, no, no, no: he painted it yellow because yellow symbolized so much for him.

Beverly (*turning the record off*) Shall we liven things up a bit?

Tony ⎫
Angela ⎭ Yeah. ⎰ (*Speaking together*)

Beverly Yeah?

Laurence Do you like Art?

Angela Yes!

Laurence *Good.* This is a Lowry! Now, did you know, his father was an estate agent?

Angela Oh.

Beverly For Christ's sake, Laurence, give it a rest!

Laurence Give what a rest?

Beverly Nobody is interested.

Laurence Oh yes, they are!

Beverly Oh no, they're not!

Laurence D'you know something, Beverly? You're ignorant!

Beverly Oh, so I'm ignorant, now, am I?

Laurence Now? You always have been!

Beverly It's not a question of ignorance, Laurence it's a question of taste!

Laurence Taste! And what would you know about taste?

Beverly The trouble with you, Laurence, is if somebody doesn't happen to like what you like, then you say that they've got no taste!

Laurence That's rubbish!

Beverly Oh, is it rubbish?

Laurence Yes!

Beverly Then what about that picture I've got upstairs in the bedroom, then?

Laurence That is cheap, pornographic trash!

Beverly Laurence, just because a picture happens to be erotic, it doesn't mean it's pornographic.

Laurence Oh, *shut up*, Beverly!

Laurence rushes to the kitchen. During the following he pours and drinks a glass of water

Beverly (*continuing immediately*) I've got this fabulous picture, right, it's really beautiful; I brought it home, and he wouldn't let me put it up in here, oh, no: I had to hang it in the bedroom!

Laurence (*from the kitchen*) If I had my way it would be in the dustbin!

Beverly Yeah, well you're dead from the waist down anyway, let's face it!

Angela Can I see it?

Beverly D'you wanna see it, Ang?

Angela Oh, yes.

Tony (*rising*) Actually, Angela's got to be getting up early in the morning for work, so I think we ought to be going now.

Susan (*rising*) Yes, I think I ought to be getting along . . .

Tony You can see the picture another time.

Laurence comes back from the kitchen

Angela We don't have to go early just 'cos of me.
Beverly You sure, Ang?
Angela Yeah, I'll be all right.
Laurence She's got to get up in the morning!
Beverly Oh, shut up, Laurence!
Laurence Don't tell me to shut up!
Tony Angela—*coat!*
Angela No, it's all right.
Susan I really think I ought to be going.
Beverly Now don't be silly, Sue, because we haven't had a cup of coffee
yet—now sit down.

Beverly exits

Laurence (*following her*) Beverly!

Laurence exits

Angela (*to Susan*) We're going soon, anyway.
Laurence (*off*) Beverly, don't bring that picture downstairs!
Beverly (*off*) Oh, sod off, Laurence!
Laurence (*off*) Beverly!
Beverly (*off*) *Drop dead!*
Tony (*to Angela*) You just can't keep your big mouth shut, can you?
Get up

Angela gets up

*Laurence enters quickly, goes to the stereo, looks for and finds a record
which he puts on the turntable, and turns on the machine*

Laurence (*during the pause before the music starts*) Sit down—please!

*Laurence sits. Angela sits. Susan sits. Tony does not sit. Laurence jumps up,
goes to look at the record, walks towards the door, stops, looks at Tony, sits,
waits. The music starts: Beethoven's Fifth Symphony, the first movement.
Laurence now suffers a heart-attack. He tries to suppress it for a time, as it
approaches, whilst the others look on, confused. Then, a spasm, and he passes
out. Angela, Susan and Tony go over to him during the following*

Angela Laurence? Laurence!
Susan What's the matter?
Tony What's wrong with him, Ang?
Angela (*examining Laurence*) Just a minute. (*She loosens his tie*)
Tony Ang, what's wrong with him?
Angela I don't know yet! (*She examines Laurence's eyes*). Tony, can you
help me get him on the floor?

*Beverly enters, displaying a picture: "The Wings of Love" by Stephen
Pearson—or some other appropriate picture*

*Angela and Tony move Laurence, helped by Susan. Throughout the following,
Angela monitors Laurence's pulse*

Get me something for his head. And get his feet up higher. No, that's
too big, give me the little one.

*Susan gets a stool or pouffe. Angela places a cushion under Laurence's
neck—not under his head*

Beverly What's going on? What's the matter with him? Mind, Sue.
Laurence! What's happened, Ang, has he passed out? Laurence!
Angela Tony, can you lift his feet?
Beverly Tony!

Tony and Susan see to Laurence's feet, placing them on the stool

Sue, go and get him a glass of water, quickly, please. Now Laurence,
come on, you're all right come on, Laurence, Laurence!
Angela No, leave him.
Tony Leave him.
Beverly Actually, Angela, he happens to be my husband, all right?
Angela Yeah, but we've got to let him breathe.
Beverly Yeh, well he is breathing, for Christ's sake.

Beverly	*(shaking him)* Laurence, come on, come on!	*(Speaking together)*
Angela	Can you get an ambulance, instead of sitting there?	

Tony Ambulance?
Angela Yes!
Susan Beverly, leave him alone!
Beverly All right, then, Angela what is the matter with him?
Angela I think he's had a heart-attack.
Tony Where's your phone?
Beverly A heart-attack, Ang?
Tony Where's your phone?
Beverly Under the bar. Ang, are you sure?

Tony goes to the telephone

Angela He hasn't got false teeth, has he?
Beverly No, of course he hasn't got false teeth! Ang, look his lips are
going all blue, look.
Angela Don't worry.
Beverly Ang, his hands are freezing.
Angela *(to Susan)* Can you get him a blanket or something to keep him
warm?

Susan exits

Beverly Laurence! Now, Laurence. Can he hear me, d'you think, Ang?
Angela Yes.
Beverly Yeah. Laurence, Laurence.

Angela No, leave him, he's got to lie still!
Beverly Oh Christ, Ang!

Beverly gets up, goes to the bar, and pours herself a brandy

Angela Have you got through yet?

Susan enters with a duvet

Tony I'm trying to get a bloody line.

Susan covers Laurence with the duvet

Beverly Ang, his face is going all blue, look!
Tony Ambulance.
Angela Tell them it's urgent.
Tony What? Someone turn that fucking record off! Er—five-oh-three nine-oh-four-one.

Susan turns off the record

Beverly Ang, Ang. Listen to that noise he's making.
Tony (*on the telephone*) Hullo, er, could we have an ambulance please? (*Pause*) What's the number of your house? What's the number of your *house!*
Susan Er—thirteen!
Beverly Thirteen, thirteen.
Tony (*on the telephone*) Thirteen Richmond Road.

For the rest of the telephone conversation that follows, Tony and Beverly overlap slightly

Beverly Angela, I told him this would happen.
Tony (*on the telephone*) Er, he's had a heart-attack.
Beverly I said to him, Laurence you're going to have a heart-attack.
Tony (*on the telephone*) Five-oh-three nine-oh-four-one.
Beverly But he wouldn't listen to me, Ang.
Tony (*on the telephone*) That's right, yeah.
Beverly But I never thought it would happen at this age; I thought it'll be more when he was fifty or sixty.
Tony (*on the telephone*) Thank you. (*He hangs up*).
Beverly Oh, Christ. Christ, Sue, listen to that noise he's making, Sue!
Susan Angela, is there anything we can do?
Angela No, we must just wait for the ambulance.

Beverly lights a cigarette

Beverly Ang, what happens when they get him to the hospital? Will they give him oxygen to revive him?
Angela They've got everything he needs in the ambulance.
Beverly Yeah?

Susan puts away the Beethoven

Oh, Christ! (*She goes back to the bar for more brandy*) Sue, d'you want a little drop of brandy?

Susan No, thank you.
Beverly Tone?
Tony No, thank you!
Beverly } Ang, d'you want a little drop of brandy? { (*Speaking*
Angela } No, no.   { *together*)
Beverly Now, Ang, listen to me—d'you think it would be a good idea if I put a little dab of brandy on his lips?
Angela No!
Beverly Now I don't mean for him to drink it—no? Well, how about a little dab of water, then, eh?
Angela No, he must just lie still.
Beverly Well, shall I get a cold flannel and lay it across his forehead?
Angela He'll be all right if he lies still.
Beverly (*kneeling*) 'Cos I am very fond of him, you know, Ang.
Tony Keep that cigarette out of his face!
Beverly All right, Tony lay off me if you don't mind, please!
Susan Beverly, you're flicking ash all over him!
Beverly All right, Sue, that'll do from you as well!
Susan Calm down!
Beverly Look, Sue—it's all right for you, your husband isn't lying here with a heart-attack, is he?
Susan Angela, is there nothing we can do?
Angela No! Just sit down.

Susan sits

Beverly It's my fault, isn't it? I know it is, Ang. But, I didn't mean to upset him tonight, I didn't, Sue, I wouldn't do that. But, Sue, he is argumentative with me. And when he shouts, I can't help but shout back; but I didn't mean to upset him tonight. You see, and when he started talking about his pictures, I should have kept quiet, but I couldn't. And I shouldn't have brought that picture down, Sue, 'cos he hates that picture. (*Pause*) Oh Christ, this is ridiculous! Tony, where's that ambulance? Ang, shall we give them a ring again?
Susan Beverly, we've only just phoned them!
Beverly I know we've only just phoned them, Sue, but you don't know what's going on at these places, they could have taken the address down wrong, or anything—they might go to the wrong road for all we know! Tony, do me a favour, get on the phone, and just check what's going on, please!
Tony Shall I ring them again, Ang?
Beverly Look, never mind her, I know she's a nurse, but I happen to be his bloody wife!
Tony All right.
Beverly Now get on the phone!

Tony dials nine-nine-nine. Beverly sits

Susan How is he?
Angela He's all right.

Beverly Mind you, Sue, he's brought this on himself. I'm sorry, but he has. If you knew, Sue, the number of times I have pleaded with him to take a day off and relax, and he wouldn't—he wouldn't listen to me, Sue. He wouldn't take any notice of me, Sue! And d'you know why? Because basically he's stubborn, and he's pig-headed!

Tony (*on the telephone*) Ambulance. Five-oh-three nine-oh-four-one. Yes.

Beverly Thirteen Richmond Road, tell 'em, Tony, and it's off Ravensway. Make sure they've got it right.

Tony (*on the telephone*) Hallo—er, we phoned for an ambulance earlier, and it doesn't seem to have arrived.

Beverly Listen, Tony, tell them we've been waiting for ten minutes actually, and there's a man lying here with a heart-attack.

Tony (*to Beverly*) Shut up!

Susan Beverly. *Be quiet!*

Beverly I beg your pardon, Sue?

Susan Will you just shut up for a minute?

Beverly Look Sue, I'm telling you now—this is my house, and if you don't like it, piss off!

Angela Oh, shut up, please.

Tony (*on the telephone*) Thirteen Richmond Road. Five-oh-three nine-oh-four-one. Ta. Thank you. (*He hangs up*).

Beverly What did they say, Tone?

Tony It's on its way.

Beverly Great.

Pause. The shrieking voices of a few teenage girls are heard in the street. Then the rock music from the party starts again

Oh, for God's sake, Sue, would you go down and tell Abigail?

Susan It's not my fault they're making such a row.

Beverly I know, Sue, but she's your daughter, isn't she?

Susan Well, I can't help that! Can I use the phone?

Beverly Yeah, go on.

Laurence starts to come round

Angela Now it's all right—just lie still.

Susan goes to the telephone and dials

Beverly What is it, Ang? Is he coming round a little bit, is he?

Angela Yeah. You're gonna be fine—keep still.

Beverly Now Laurence—Laurence, it's Beverly speaking! Now, listen to me, Laurence. I'm just putting me cigarette down—

At about this point, Laurence dies. Unaware of this Beverly continues to speak; Angela starts to pound his chest towards the end of her speech

—'cos we don't want to blow smoke in your face, do we? Now, listen to me, Laurence. Now Laurence, you're not well. You're gonna be all right, we're gonna take you to the hospital—now listen to me—I'm gonna stay with you all the time, Laurence, and I'm not gonna leave you,

all right? Now Ang is looking after you, see? (*As Angela pounds Laurence's chest*) Ang! Ang, what're you doing?
Susan (*on the telephone*) Could I speak to Abigail, please? Abigail! Abigail Lawson! . . .

Angela listens to Laurence's chest. She starts to administer the kiss-of-life. Then she stops

Angela Tony, can you hold my hair out of my face?
Tony Eh?
Angela Tony!

Tony goes and holds Angela's hair out of the way, whilst she does the kiss-of-life. This goes on for some time. Eventually, she gives up. Tony lets go of her hair. She sinks back against an armchair. Pause. Beverly throws her arms round Tony with a gasp, holding the embrace. Pause. Angela leaps up suddenly, grasping one leg

Ur, shit! Ur, Tony, Tony. Tony!

Angela flies across the room. Tony disengages himself from Beverly

Tony What's the matter? You haven't got cramp again, have you? Come here—give us your leg! Stretch it. Stretch it!

Angela is relieved, and lies still on the floor. Tony kneels in exhaustion. Beverly sobs

Susan (*on the telephone*) Abigail, it's Mummy here . . . Abigail? . . . Abigail! . . .

The Lights fade to a Black-out and the rock music surges, as—

the CURTAIN *falls*

FURNITURE AND PROPERTY LIST

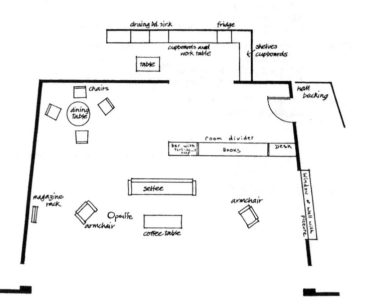

ACT I

On stage: LIVING-ROOM

Leather 3-piece suite. *On it:* cushions
Pouffe
Dining-table. *On it:* candelabra
4 dining-chairs
Coffee-table. *On it:* cigarette-box, lighter, ashtray, copy of "Cosmo-politan"
Magazine rack. *In it:* various magazines
Room-divider. *On it:* **Beverly's** handbag with bottle of perfume, telephone, automatic stereo system with records, ornamental fibre-light, fold-down desk, bar. *In bar section:* whisky, sherry, brandy, vodka, gin, tonic water, Bacardi, Coca Cola, light ale, soda-water, ice bowl, sliced lemon, openers, assorted glasses
Bookshelves. *In them:* books, including modern sets of Dickens and Shakespeare, dressing
On walls: various prints, including a Van Gogh and a Lowry
Sheepskin rug
Carpet

KITCHEN

(Note: if necessary, much of the kitchen can be presumed off-stage, and some of the following items out of sight)

Refrigerator. *In it:* 2 small plates of cheese-and-pineapple savouries with cocktail-sticks, dressing

Table. *On it:* tray of crisps and salted peanuts

Fitments and cupboards. *In and on them:* crockery, cutlery, jar of olives, dressing

Rôtisserie

Sink with practical tap. *On it:* soap, towel, dressing

Off stage: Executive case with papers, notebook, antacid tablets, cigars **(Laurence)**
Wrapped bottle of Beaujolais **(Susan)**
Carrier bag with lager beer **(Laurence)**

Personal: **Susan:** handbag. *In it:* tissues
Angela: handbag

ACT II

Set: In kitchen: cup of black coffee, kitchen knife, bread, tub of margarine, sandwich filling

Off stage: Picture **(Beverly)**
Duvet **(Susan)**

LIGHTING PLOT

Property fittings required: wall brackets, kitchen fitment, fibre-light
Interior. A living-room and kitchen. The same scene throughout

ACT I	Early Evening	
To open:	Black-out	
Cue 1	As CURTAIN rises *Bring up lighting to overall effect of early spring evening daylight*	(Page 1)
Cue 2	**Angela** (*off*): "Better out than in." *Fade to Black-out for Curtain*	(Page 31)
ACT II	A little later	
To open:	All interior lighting on	
Cue 3	**Susan:** "Abigail? . . . Abigail! . . ." *Fade to Black-out for Curtain*	(Page 54)

EFFECTS PLOT

ACT I

Cue 1   **Beverly** starts record-player   (Page 1)
After pause, bring up music: Donna Summer—"Love to Love you, Baby"

Cue 2   **Laurence** turns down volume   (Page 1)
Reduce music volume

Cue 3   **Beverly:** ". . . put them out, please?"   (Page 3)
Front doorbell chimes

Cue 4   **Angela:** "Thanks."   (Page 10)
Front doorbell chimes

Cue 5   **Beverly:** "Yes. Great"   (Page 13)
Rock music starts from neighbouring house. This continues, intermittently, throughout the Act

Cue 6   **Beverly:** ". . . a little top-up. That's it."   (Page 28)
Music: José Feliciano—"California Dreamin' "

Cue 7   **Beverly** turns volume up   (Page 30)
Bring up volume on track following previous number, "Light my Fire"

Cue 8   **Laurence** turns off record-player   (Page 30)
Snap off music

ACT II

Cue 9   As Curtain rises   (Page 32)
Rock music as in Act I, continues as before

Cue 10   After **Laurence** exits to kitchen   (Page 37)
Front doorbell chimes

Cue 11   **Beverly:** "Ready, Ang?"   (Page 39)
Music: Elvis Presley—"Don't"

Cue 12   **Laurence** turns down volume   (Page 39)
Reduce music level

Cue 13   **Beverly** turns up volume   (Page 42)
Increase music level—snap off as Laurence stops record

Cue 14   **Beverly:** "Ready, Ang?"   (Page 44)
Music: Sam-the Man-Taylor—"Blue Mist" (see note on recordings)

Cue 15   **Beverly** turns down volume   (Page 44)
Reduce music level

| *Cue* 16 | **Beverly** turns off record-player | (Page 48) |
| | *Snap off music* | |

Cue 17   **Laurence** moves to door, returns, sits   (Page 49)
*Pause, then music from record-player of Beethoven's
Fifth Symphony*

Cue 18   **Susan** turns record off   (Page 51)
Snap off music

Cue 19   **Tony:** "It's on its way."   **Beverly:** "Great."   (Page 53)
*Pause, then shrieks of teenage girls from nearby. In-
crease rock music*

Cue 20   As CURTAIN falls   (Page 54)
Rock music increases further

NOTE ON RECORDINGS

1. "Love to Love you, Baby" (Donna Summer):
   GTO Records. GTLP 008, Side One

2. "California Dreamin' " (José Feliciano):
   RCA Victor SF 7946, Side One Track One
   (moving on to "Light My Fire")

3. "Don't" (Elvis Presley):
   ELVIS'S 40 GREATEST
   Arcade Records ADE P 12, Record One, Side Two, Track One

4. "Blue Mist" (Sam—the Man—Taylor):
   MGM Records—USA—E/3973, Side One, Track One—
   "Harlem Nocturne" (Any "smoochy" music may be substituted)

5. Fifth Symphony (Beethoven), First Movement, any recording

MADE AND PRINTED IN GREAT BRITAIN BY
LATIMER TREND & COMPANY LTD PLYMOUTH
MADE IN ENGLAND